(MOSTLY) PRAISE FOR *SHTICK TO BUSINESS*

David Ogilvy once said, "The best ideas come as jokes. Try to make your thinking as funny as possible."

Every ruler needs a court jester. Humour is anything but silly: it is an evolved and highly sophisticated evolutionary mechanism which allows brains momentarily to sidestep conventional hierarchies or assumptions in a way which would be impossible in a wholly serious (or automated) world. In today's over-earnest business culture, where it often pays to present oneself as being as Teutonically rational as possible, it is easy to disregard these momentary logical lapses. But, as Peter McGraw explains, we should often cherish them instead.

—RORY SUTHERLAND, VICE CHAIRMAN, OGILVY

When I read the quote about me in this book, "Neal lacks the warmth that helps an audience connect to a stand-up comedian," you can imagine my excitement about endorsing it. I do endorse it. Not warmly. You know how I am.

—̃MEDIAN AND
LLE'S SHOW

D1468967

Shtick to Business takes insights from the world's funniest people to show you all you need to know about business.

Great comedians are constantly selling themselves, improving their product based on customer feedback, and differentiating themselves from the competition. Who cares if they sleep until noon & drink too much?

Let successful comedians show you their secrets to success.

—JIMMY CARR, COMEDIAN AND MAN
WHO OWES THE AUTHOR MONEY

I've built a career on creating innovation designed to disrupt markets. Peter McGraw asserts that the best case studies are not entrepreneurs like me, but T-shirt-wearing comedians working in dingy basements. I couldn't agree with him more. *Shtick to Business* is not only a fascinating deep dive into the psychology of the world's most creative minds, but also an exhaustive guide to applying those lessons to your business. A must-read for those looking to drive growth, progress, and sustainable success.

—JOSH LINKNER, 5X TECH ENTREPRENEUR,
NEW YORK TIMES BESTSELLING AUTHOR

Shtick to Business will help you think differently, build critical professional skills, and make you laugh all at the same time. Get ready to learn from professional comedians, the all-out rebels who—in many ways—have the toughest job in the world.

—FRANCESCA GINO, AUTHOR OF *REBEL TALENT* AND HARVARD BUSINESS SCHOOL PROFESSOR

Those who can, make people laugh. Those who can't, become humor researchers. Yes, that's a thing, and Peter McGraw is one of the best on the planet. Defying all expectations, his book is illuminating, entertaining, and maybe even useful.

—ADAM GRANT, *NEW YORK TIMES* BESTSELLING AUTHOR OF *ORIGINALS* AND *GIVE AND TAKE*, AND HOST OF THE TED PODCAST *WORKLIFE*

Peter McGraw is brilliant! His unique research and knowledge of behavioral science and corporate success illuminates the skills that allow the funniest entertainers and smartest businesses to succeed. Prepare to bump your career and company to 11 in this comedic book for an all too serious world.

—JON LEVY, FOUNDER OF THE INFLUENCERS AND AUTHOR OF *THE 2 AM PRINCIPLE*

Comedy is funny, but it's also a serious business that some of the best comedians turn into billion-dollar empires. No one understands this better than Peter McGraw, a serious academic who also happens to know a lot about comedy, comedians, and what makes them funny. In *Shtick to Business*, McGraw explains why comedians like Jerry Seinfeld, Tina Fey, and Amy Poehler are so successful in comedy and in business—and explains how the rest of us, funny or not, can use the same principles to sharpen our own business instincts.

—ADAM ALTER, *NEW YORK TIMES* BESTSELLING
AUTHOR OF *DRUNK TANK PINK* AND *IRRESISTIBLE*
AND ASSOCIATE PROFESSOR OF MARKETING, NEW
YORK UNIVERSITY STERN SCHOOL OF BUSINESS

Peter McGraw is THE expert on what makes us laugh. Funnily enough, he's a behavioral scientist who studies humor in business. He brings scientific understanding to creativity and innovation in the economy. No one can give better advice on how to develop your own unique creativity to succeed professionally, whether you are on stage or in the office.

—WENDY WOOD, PROFESSOR OF PSYCHOLOGY
AND BUSINESS AT THE UNIVERSITY OF
SOUTHERN CALIFORNIA AND AUTHOR
OF *GOOD HABITS, BAD HABITS*

Is Peter McGraw a superb scientist who happens to be unusually funny? Or a superb comedian who happens to be unusually scientific?

Why choose? Pete is an enlightening entertainer and an entertaining enlightener.

—PHILIP TETLOCK, ANNENBERG UNIVERSITY
PROFESSOR, UNIVERSITY OF PENNSYLVANIA,
AND AUTHOR OF *SUPERFORECASTING: THE
ART AND SCIENCE OF PREDICTION*

A book for business people who are sick of being average. McGraw delivers more insights about human behavior and leadership in two chapters than in the last five years' worth of business books combined.

—SHANE SNOW, AUTHOR OF *DREAM TEAMS*

The person who tells you that business has to be boring probably isn't very good at business. *Shtick to Business* shows how the world's funniest people can actually teach us a lot about how we can do business better. An entertaining road map that will make you smarter.

—JONAH BERGER, WHARTON PROFESSOR AND
AUTHOR OF *CONTAGIOUS* AND *THE CATALYST*

SHTICK
_to_ BUSINESS

WHAT THE MASTERS OF COMEDY
CAN TEACH YOU ABOUT
BREAKING RULES,
BEING FEARLESS, AND
BUILDING A SERIOUS CAREER

PETER McGRAW

co-author of _THE HUMOR CODE_

LIONCREST
PUBLISHING

SHTICK TO BUSINESS

What the Masters of Comedy Can Teach You about Breaking Rules, Being Fearless, and Building a Serious Career

ISBN   978-1-5445-0807-8 *Paperback*
      978-1-5445-0806-1 *Ebook*
      978-1-5445-0808-5 *Audiobook*

For the jokers, raconteurs, and other misfits
who are serious about not being serious.
Thank you for helping me think differently.
And to my sister, Shannon, who thinks
I am the funniest person on the planet.
(My words. Not hers.)

CONTENTS

INTRODUCTION 13

1. REVERSE IT 37

    ACT OUT: NOT ONE. NOT TWO. THREE. 60

2. STEP OUT OF THE STREAM 63

    ACT OUT: THIRD THOUGHTS 111

3. CREATE A CHASM.................................... 113

    ACT OUT: AN AUDIENCE OF ONE 148

4. COOPERATE TO INNOVATE 153

    ACT OUT: SUCCESS BY 1,000 CUTS 199

5. WRITE IT OR REGRET IT............................. 205

    ACT OUT: START STRONG. END STRONGER... 230

6. WORK HARD OR HARDLY WORK.................... 233

    ACT OUT: TURN DOWN THE LIGHTS.............. 269

7. TAKE A BIGGER STAGE 277

    ACT OUT: GETTING FROM YES TO NO 303

    EPILOGUE.. 307

    ACKNOWLEDGMENTS 317

    ABOUT THE AUTHOR................................. 321

INTRODUCTION

On the first day of class, I am greeted by first-year MBA students poised to climb the corporate ladder or pitch their billion-dollar idea on the next season of *Shark Tank*.

I set my briefcase beside the podium, look into their eager eyes, and say, "Business is hard. Business is hard. Business is hard."

I then watch a mix of amusement and disappointment wash over the class.

I'm *not* joking more than I'm joking. Business is hard. It is hard to produce products that delight customers, it is hard to create communications that cut through the clutter, and it is hard to develop and manage a career.

Depending on how you measure it, failure rates in business are 90 percent, 95 percent, even 99 percent—a lot like my dating life (depending on how you measure it). Even when a business is on top, it's tough to stay there. In 2018, Apple was the most innovative company in the world. Now it sits at number seventeen. And I hate to ruin your day, but there's always a recession right around the corner. (Hire me for your motivational needs!)

To top it all off, my students—and you—will soon face twice the competition. While human-versus-human competition is the norm on *Shark Tank*, soon you'll face a greater foe: a machine.

Of course, the machines won't look like those in Arnold Schwarzenegger's 1984 sci-fi classic *The Terminator*, or like Agent Smith in *The Matrix*, or like *Westworld*'s Dolores Abernathy. It will simply be a bunker filled with nameless, faceless computer servers who don't fight over the corner office.

The industrial revolution is in its fourth phase. The first phase introduced the steam engine. The second, electricity. The third radically changed the world with digital communication. (Hit me up on Instagram.) The fourth phase goes by many names: robots, computers, algorithms, artificial intelligence. For our purposes, I'll call it AI.

Most people haven't caught on to the fact that computers are catching up to most people. AI is already outperforming humans in many complex tasks. In 1996, AI used brute computing force to defeat chess grandmasters. About ten years later, a complex learning algorithm beat a world champion Go player. Go is an ancient Chinese game—likely the most complicated board game ever invented. The computer program won by making moves it had never "seen" before.

Technology has been taking jobs for a hundred years. But in previous phases of the industrial revolution, blue-collar jobs, such as farming and factory work, were most at risk.

Now AI is coming for white-collar jobs—often highly skilled work. In a test that pitted lawyers against AI to identify problems in a contract, for example, the lawyers scored 85 percent on average, and the fastest lawyer finished in fifty-one minutes. The algorithm, on the other hand, scored 94 percent in a mere twenty-six seconds. Most pharmacy work can also be done faster and more accurately by AI. Even radiologists are losing their jobs. AI never misreads an x-ray because it is distracted by its divorce proceedings.

Alexa taught me all of this when I asked her when the machines are taking over.

In short, business is hard, and it's getting harder. With

increased competition, it's less and less about how you will beat out the other meat sacks on the job market. Now it's about how you'll beat out the AI that can fix a contract, read your CAT scan, and destroy you at Go—all before you can even get dressed in the morning.

How do you stand a chance against that?

The answer: by doing things that computers can't.

COMPUTERS CAN'T FART

AI's strength is also its weakness.

AI's advantage in the marketplace is its ability to learn rules and apply them consistently. But AI can't break rules—and it can't break wind. As a result, guess who will be the last person to lose their job to the AI revolution?

That's right. The world's least-professional professionals: comedians.

Comedy is the gold standard used to evaluate AI. Computer scientists are constantly inventing and refining joke-telling algorithms. It turns out that making people laugh is so incredibly complex and nuanced, if a computer can be programmed to do it, it can do nearly everything else.

Nevertheless, AI's comedy successes are, well, laughable—limited to simple quips, wordplay, and puns. Good comedy, however, includes more than joke-telling—just look at Charlie Chaplin and Buster Keaton's silent films. A computer can't produce physical gags and can't create satire. Even the most ambitious sci-fi film has yet to imagine robots roasting each other.

Not only that, but *context* matters in comedy. Tell a baker that he has "Nice buns," and you get a laugh. Tell a banker the same thing, and you get a lawsuit.

Comedians don't care about lawsuits; they care about laughs. Great comedy is based on novelty, and so comedy as a craft is constantly evolving—faster than businesses innovate. Starbucks can sell you the same pumpkin spice latte day in and day out, but a stand-up comedian can't tell the same joke to the same audience twice.

At first blush, comedy seems to be solely a talent game: you either have "it" or you don't. Sure, good instincts and natural ability matter, but becoming a master of comedy takes a commitment to professional development with a focus on creativity and a whole lot of work. It also takes time. You can earn an MBA in two years, but it takes ten years to get good at comedy—ten years of breaking rules, being fearless, and building the career skills needed on and off the stage or screen.

It's not just the masters of comedy who know the importance of skill development for success. Based on the threat of AI, a 2018 World Economic Forum report forecasts the top skills for the forthcoming workforce. Oddly, it's the odd-numbered skills on the list that I want to bring attention to: 1) Analytical thinking and innovation, 3) Creativity, originality, and initiative, 5) Critical thinking and analysis, 7) Leadership and social influence, 9) Reasoning, problem-solving, and ideation.[1]

These skills also happen to be the hallmark of successful comedians. Everything about what they do, and how they do it well, requires that they be masters of these skills.

Now, for some of you, the above view of the AI takeover is overly pessimistic. I get it. I'm also an optimist by nature. Here's the positive spin. The odd-numbered creative skills are still important because a whole lot of new jobs will be created because of AI. Technological advances create new jobs. Because of the digital revolution, for example, we now have Uber drivers, Airbnb hosts, and Kim Kardashian.

In any case, my contention is clear. By emulating the funniest people, you can craft a better career and a smarter business.

---

1   World Economic Forum (2018). The Future of Jobs: Employment, Skills and Workforce Strategy for the Fourth Industrial Revolution.

All without telling a joke.

WHY ARE WE LAUGHING?

To understand how to apply the distinguishing character-
istics of comedy to business, you should understand some
basics about humor. Here's a crash course in comedy
theory.

I started out as a typical academic. As a marketing and
psychology professor, I teach business students behavioral economics, consumer behavior, advertising, and
marketing management. I've done well enough that business schools fly me in to teach their MBAs.

But like many good jokes (and new business innovations),
my life had an unexpected twist. During the first half of
my career, I spent a lot of time doing behavioral economics research. I answered questions like, "How do feelings
affect the ways people spend money?" "Can people feel
happy and sad at the same time?" And, "Why does the
TSA suck?"

More than a decade ago, while conducting studies on
moral judgment and decision-making, I was invited by
a fellow professor and co-author to give a talk at her university—a common practice in the world of academia. In
exchange for a flight, hotel room, and a delicious meal, an

academic audience gets an early look at your research and craps on your ideas for an hour. Unlike getting blocked on Twitter by your nemesis, it's an honor you get to put on your curriculum vitae.

In the talk, I presented our latest research examining the morality of religious marketing. At the time, evangelical churches had started using marketing tactics to save lost souls. Like a good business, they sought consumer insights: why don't people come to church? The feedback: the sermon puts me to sleep, my kids are bored to tears, and parking is hell. The church's solution: add a rock band, hire valets, and add "entertainment" centers with video games and coffee bars.

I shared an anecdote with these professors about a Tampa church that used a promotion to increase attendance to its winter retreat: anyone who showed up to the retreat was entered into a raffle to win prizes. For some members of the public, this alone was abhorrent, but for others, it was the church's particularly conspicuous grand prize that crossed the line: a yellow H2 Hummer SUV.

My research predicted that the audience would be upset, but this was not the case. They laughed. Granted, it wasn't a full-on guffaw—more like a hearty giggle. A hand went up in the back of the room. One of the professors who had been quiet to that point asked me the most important question of my life:

> You just told us how moral violations create anger and disgust. And yet when you presented a moral violation to us, we laughed. Why?

I stood there completely dumbfounded. For the first time, I wondered: *What makes things funny?*

WHAT MAKES THINGS FUNNY

Understanding humor is important.

Humor is a universal experience for people of all ages and cultures. There's even evidence that mammals—including chimps, dogs, and even rats—have their own animal versions of laughter when engaged in rough and tumble play.[2]

The pursuit of humor influences who we choose to spend time with. We gravitate to people who make us laugh or who laugh at our jokes. Pro tip: If you and another person are laughing at the same thing, you likely have a lot in common. Humor is such a powerful social tool that

---

2   Ask dog owners whether their dog has a sense of humor, and you will get enthusiastic stories. Cat owners...not so much.

people often fake a laugh—which explains your boss's delusional self-confidence.

The pursuit of humor also motivates how we spend our money and our time: the talk radio and podcasts we listen to, the Twitter and Instagram accounts we follow, and the television and movies we watch.

The question of what makes things funny happens to date back at least two-and-a-half millennia to Greek philosophy. Aristotle and Plato puzzled over this question, as well as other great minds in philosophy, social sciences, and entertainment: Thomas Hobbes, Immanuel Kant, Charles Darwin, Sigmund Freud, Mark Twain, Carol Burnett, Judd Apatow, and Johnny Knoxville.

Despite not being one of history's great thinkers, I had two critical advantages. One, I could stand on their shoulders. Two, I had the ability to run experiments.

I can plan an experiment and analyze data like a champ (that is, if there were championships for data analysis). However, I didn't believe I could tackle this question alone. So I enlisted a super-smart PhD student, Caleb Warren. Our initial goal was modest: explain when people laugh at moral violations. To answer that question, we had to figure out the answer to the bigger question of what makes things funny. The problem was that the study of humor was relegated to a niche group of researchers—none of whom I had ever heard of.

We found a paper in an obscure journal by Thomas Veatch, a linguist. I believed it to be the best writing on the topic, and Caleb and I worked to further Veatch's ideas into what we call the Benign Violation Theory.

BENIGN VIOLATION THEORY

A benign violation is a paradoxical situation in which something is wrong, threatening, or confusing (a violation), yet simultaneously okay, safe, or makes sense (benign). The resulting laughter says to the world, "That thing that seems wrong is actually okay." In the case of tickling and rough and tumble play, these are harmless attacks.[3]

The theory explains the two ways that humor attempts fail. If a situation is solely a violation, it produces outrage and disgust. If the situation is solely benign, it produces boredom. To be funny, it takes a precise mix of both—the sweet spot in the center. No easy task.

---

3   Physical comedy has the same elements. In other words, the first comedian was likely a monkey, which makes the slipping on the banana peel bit a lot older than you'd think.

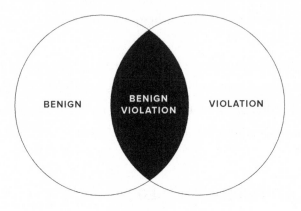

In wordplay, for example, something might convey a meaning that is naughty from one perspective yet nice from another perspective. This is precisely why "Nice buns" is funny to a baker (benign violation) but harassment to the banker (pure violation).

The theory also explains the well-known saying that Comedy = Tragedy + Time. This is why you often hear the phrase "too soon" when Gilbert Gottfried or Anthony Jeselnik make a joke on social media immediately after a tragedy.[4]

Proximity—whether through time, physical distance, or social connection—affects how amusing something

4   When there is a tragedy, Anthony Jeselnik's friends and family immediately text him, "Don't do it!"

can be. The farther away, the more benign. The closer, the greater the threat of the violation. For example, it is not funny when your child falls off a skateboard, but it might be funny when you see someone *else* do it, especially someone you *don't* know, on YouTube. The multiple forms of distance help the accident land in that sweet spot of the Venn diagram.[5]

And if the skateboarder is a stranger who trash-talked a homeless person before taking a nosedive ass over teakettle, well that's even better because that clown deserved it.

Here is one last bit of evidence. This theory also explains why the very same joke can be perceived so differently by three different people: benign (boring) versus a violation (offensive) versus a benign violation (funny). What's funny (or not) is subjective to you the individual: your values, culture, mood, and the number of drinks you had. This is precisely what makes comedy so difficult, and why we value it so highly—especially when people can do it on command.

BUT WHAT DO I KNOW?

I may be just another meat sack, but I've spent long days and nights stuck in my office writing esoteric research

---

5   By the way, if my warnings about AI takeover were too much of a violation, look up robot fails on YouTube, enjoy a laugh, and get sense of relief.

papers about the causes and consequences of humor (that's Dr. Meat Sack, thank you very much). To facilitate my academic research, I even founded the Humor Research Lab, affectionately known as HuRL.[6]

My papers were being accepted into the foremost scientific journals, and I was starting to feel a little too good about myself. So good, in fact, that in a moment of hubris I tried stand-up...at an open mic...at a dive bar... and *bombed*.

I'm not kidding—I got one laugh, it was unintentional, and it wasn't because I was wearing a sweater vest.

Turns out that bombing was beneficial. I realized that to fully understand the complexity of humor, I had to tussle with the messiness of comedy in the real world.

I teamed up with Joel Warner, a Denver-based journalist, to go on a quixotic global expedition to crack the humor code.

The experience changed my perspective—and my life. I witnessed a sketch comedy show get shut down by the

---

6 My decision to study humor is seen as frivolous by many academic peers. I once gave a talk about my research at an Ivy League B-school. Afterwards, I met with one of the professors. As I waited for the run-of-the-mill, "I enjoyed your talk" conversation, he casually leaned back in his leather chair and said, "I am impressed, what you are doing with this humor thing. It's a career killer."

Palestinian government, investigated the causes of the Muhammed cartoon controversy in Denmark, examined a laughter epidemic in Tanzania, clowned with Patch Adams in the Amazon, got shitfaced with Mad Men in New York, traded wisecracks with comedians on a Japanese game show, and studied with the world's best improvisers at Upright Citizens Brigade (UCB) in Los Angeles.

After 91,000 miles crisscrossing the globe, Joel and I had plenty of material for our book, *The Humor Code*. And because he is always looking for an entertaining story, Joel made me perform stand-up again—this time at the Just for Laughs Festival, the largest comedy stage on the planet.

Fortunately, that attempt went better than the first time. But believe me, for the sake of the world and comedy club audiences everywhere, I decided to focus on studying comedy instead of performing it.

THREE PILLARS OF COMEDY

The lessons in this book have been gleaned from countless hours observing, discussing, researching, and attempting comedy—in all its forms. I spend a lot of time with comedians, many of whom have become my friends, confidants, and business partners. To that end, I host *I'm*

Not Joking, a podcast which looks at the lives of funny people. And for fun, I created a comedy game show called *Funny or True?* which pits comedians against scientists to see who has the best blend of brains and funny bone.

From all these avenues of studying comedy, I find that most professional opportunities in comedy fall into three categories:

Stand-up. Stand-up is what most people think of when they hear the words comedy or comedian: a single person standing on a stage, delivering rehearsed material to a captive audience. Stand-up comedians are very good at pointing out what is wrong with the world in a way that delights (and usually doesn't offend) the audience in front of them. Many of the comedy case studies in this book are drawn from this world.

Improv. Improvisational comedy formulates funny out of nothingness. I'll say it again, nothingness. Improv is comedy born out of a kernel of an idea, unplanned and unrehearsed. The art form is fascinatingly less focused on the audience and more focused on the improv team. If the team functions well, laughs follow. Improv is about innovation.

Sketch. Sketch comedy integrates the writing that under-lies stand-up and the cooperation of an improv team.

Sketch is the basis for sitcoms and movie scenes. Not only are there usually multiple writers in sketch comedy, but there is also a director who translates a script into action and actors who translate what the director wants into actions, perhaps improvising to improve the final product.

Each pillar has best practices and intense perspectives. Yes, comedians may drink too much and wear cargo shorts to work, but they make a difficult job look easy. This is precisely why I want you to pay attention to how they do their job so you can get ahead in the serious world of business.

LESSONS FOR BUSINESS

When I started studying humor, I thought I was leaving my business professor life behind. But as I got to know comedy, the business professor in me couldn't help but notice the practices, perspectives, and personalities that led some comedians to succeed and others to fail.

Through the combination of my worlds—business, science, and comedy—I will present unique insights that get to the heart of what it takes to be successful.

Look for these elements in each chapter:

Comedy. Each chapter contains a glimpse into the entertaining yet mysterious world of professional comedy. You won't get the same old stories that you see in every other business or self-help book. Instead, you'll learn:

- The most important lie that Jamie Foxx ever told.
- How Hannah Gadsby became more famous when she stopped telling jokes.
- Why Andy Kaufman got himself fired from a TV show for a comedy bit.
- How Doug Stanhope turned a crime into a stand-up special.
- Why Joan Rivers' card catalog of jokes rivaled the Library of Congress.
- The one tool every comedian carries at all times. (And no, it isn't a bong.)

Commerce. Besides pulling back the curtain on the habits of the world's funniest people, you will also receive actionable lessons to apply to your professional life. Get ready to overcome your professional challenges by learning:

- A simple "101" comedy trick used by Chris Rock, Tina Fey, and nearly every other comedian that will help you overcome biases and generate better business solutions.
- How the cooperative model of *SNL* and *In Living Color* can elevate your team and turn an idea into a profitable product.

- How the hidden magic of comedy club design can inform the ultimate UX.
- Why a constraint used by the writers of *The Onion* can enhance your creativity.
- The essential lesson of Bill Murray's 1-800 number—and why saying "no" is often more important than saying "yes."

Evidence. There will be support from cutting-edge behavioral sciences, business research, and real-world case studies. I'll spare you most of the academic jargon, but just know that I was wearing a lab coat when I wrote these parts.

Implications and Takeaways. Every lesson has the potential for direct application, and I've designed specific tasks to help you do just that. Some will be at the end of the chapter under "Implication" or "Develop Your Shtick." Others can be found at PeterMcGraw.org, where you can download a free workbook with practice exercises.

Act Outs. In between chapters, I have included mini-lessons from the masters of comedy. Look for these "act outs" as a palate cleanser of sorts.

Entertainment. People should expect a book about comedy to be funny. Yes, we'll have some laughs, but more importantly, I want to make sure that your career isn't a joke. As a bonus, I have created a YouTube play-list for many of the referenced comedy bits and other resources.

More importantly, I've enlisted my good friend Shane Mauss, who will show up from time to time to share insights from his life as a professional comedian. While I'm a scientist who studies comedy, he's a comedian who jokes about science. Naturally, we're friends. And because he doesn't work at a university, he can say things that I can't.

Look for Shane's "Shtick Figure" that signals he's about to weigh in with his comedic POV.

SHTICK FROM SHANE

As Pete mentioned, he and I are a bit of an odd couple. Drastically different people, in such wonderfully compatible ways.

I make people laugh. Pete laughs easily. He's a scientist, and I've drunk out of beakers. When we met, I was a wild party animal, and Pete was...well...Pete was wearing a sweater vest.

I was beginning to explore science through comedy (something most comedy audiences have no interest in), and Pete was beginning to explore comedy through science (something most academics have no interest in). We'd both had success in our traditional roles and were taking risks stepping into the unknown with no guarantees it would pay off.

A promising setup.

As someone who considers himself a student of the craft and has spent a lot of time really analyzing and thinking deeply about what makes good comedy, I love what Pete does. And he is shockingly good at it.

There are far too many people out there (comedians included) who think comedy is some innate gift that can't be taught or studied. They're the type of people who refuse to read the instructions when assembling Ikea furniture. Sure, that looks like a bookcase, but I wouldn't put my forthcoming Pulitzer Prize for this book on it.

Don't be that person. Read the instructions.

Thanks, Shane. By the way, I did not pay him to say that. In fact, he's not getting paid at all. I hope he knows that.

DON'T TRY TO BE FUNNIER AT WORK

To be perfectly clear: this is not a book about being humorous in order to get ahead in business. I once argued for the benefits of humor in the workplace. However, I changed my mind.

I simply don't believe that being funny is the best solution to most people's professional problems.

First, the risks of humor in a business setting aren't necessarily worth the potential rewards. There are twice as many ways to fail than succeed. Comedy can fail by: 1) boring people to death, or 2) causing outrage and social isolation. And it's tough to predict which way you will fail.

Second, laughs are a moving target. While humor is a universal experience, what is benign and what is a violation (i.e., what is funny) are ridiculously subjective and based on vast individual and cultural differences. In short, the same joke can make one person laugh, another person yawn, and yet another person gasp.

Third, everyone thinks they're funny because they are *to

themselves. Some people are truly funny, but the average joke teller relies on what he or she finds funny rather than what the audience will find funny. So, if I tell everyone to be funny, we need to worry about "that guy." The guy who thinks he's funny (but isn't). Like my students often remind me after I crack a joke...the workplace doesn't need "that guy."

Fourth, even when you are successfully funny, comedy can still backfire. For example, a recent study found that making jokes during a presentation enhances a man's status but hurts a woman's status.[7] SMH.

You may become funnier as you learn the comedic lessons herein. But if you want to be funnier at work, take an improv class. Or take a chance on a book designed to teach you how to be funny. Don't blame me if being the comedian in the office doesn't result in a standing ovation. I'm trying to get you promoted up the ranks, not called down to HR.

---

7   Evans, J. B., Slaughter, J. E., Ellis, A. P. J., & Rivin, J. M. (2019). Gender and the evaluation of humor at work, *Journal of Applied Psychology, 104*, 1077-1087.

SHTICK FROM SHANE

If you are wondering if you should tell a comedian a joke, you shouldn't.

At the end of my shows, I often have excited audience members approach me. Some compliment me. Some buy a T-shirt. On occasion, in an effort to *help me* someone will say, "You probably hate when people say to you 'I have a joke for you.'"

I'll respond, "Yes."

Then they will say, "Well, I have a joke for you."

I then brace myself for the most racist yet strangely boring joke I've heard since middle school.

SHTICK TO BUSINESS

Whether you want to launch a company, get a promotion, or fight the AI takeover, emulating the skills of the masters of comedy can revolutionize your work life—and beyond.

Remember, I don't want you to be funny. I want you to *think* funny. That is, I want you to start thinking differently. Thus, I will never ask you to tell a joke in order to apply one of my lessons.

Can comedy save the world—or at least the business world?

Let's find out.

CHAPTER 1

REVERSE IT

"We need bullies."

Chris Rock shares this unsettling perspective in his Netflix stand-up comedy special, *Tambourine*. He describes the strict no-bullying policy at his daughter's school, one so strict that any bully will be kicked out of school immediately.

His response?

"And right then, I wanted to take my daughter out of the school."

Chris Rock has written, produced, directed, and starred in movies and television, but he is best known for his stand-up. His comedy specials *Bring the Pain* and *Bigger and Blacker* made him a household name (and one of my favorite comedians). He developed his delivery style by observing his father and grandfather, both preachers. Rock paces the stage, repeats his premise, and often stops suddenly for emphasis. He even has his own catchphrase, "Yeah, I said it!"

Rock believes the world is better with bullies. Bullies prepare children for the harsh realities of adulthood. "Bullies do half the work. That's right. Teachers do one-half, bullies do the whole other half. And that's the half you're going to use."

He points out that, sure, you may know how to program a computer, but that doesn't matter much if "you start crying because your boss didn't say 'Hi.'"

He closes with this bit of wisdom: "Pressure makes diamonds. Not hugs."

Sure, bullies are bad, but Chris Rock makes a compelling case for the opposite. He is a master of the reversal.

SMASH THE STATUS QUO

Chris Rock, like most comedians, is no fan of the status quo.

Comedians are constantly looking for what's wrong with

the way things are. They seem to recognize what most people (and businesses) don't: the status quo is something to be loathed and avoided at *all costs*.

Most of the time, people seek to maintain the status quo. No big changes. Let's not get crazy. The desire to cling to the status quo and avoid change is so pervasive and problematic, scientists have given it a name: the status quo bias.

Behavioral economists, entrepreneurs, and CEOs are (or at least should be) particularly concerned about the status quo bias because it inhibits risk-taking and disguises opportunities. People with this bias (in other words, most of humanity) find it exceptionally difficult to move away from their current state of the world. The bias makes change difficult, so things stay the same.

The underlying cause of the bias is loss aversion: the loss of a change looms larger than the gain from the change. Basically, we are more sensitive to potentially bad things than potentially good things. Have you ever started a new job and made a suggested change only to hear the response, "That's not how we do it here"? You have just witnessed the status quo bias in action.

Thinking in reverse creates a path that deviates from the status quo in a direction that few people are thinking. It often makes people uncomfortable. But extraordinary results do not come from ordinary thinking.

HARDCORE FOR YOUR HEALTH

You know who else is no fan of the status quo? Tony Horton.[8]

For decades, the status quo in the fitness industry was to sell "easy" ways to get in shape. ThighMaster. Vibro-belts. Sauna suits. Jazzercise. Toning Shoes. 8-minute abs. 7-minute abs. 6-minute abs. 5-minute abs. You get the point.

And the Shake Weight.

The Shake Weight is a ridiculous product. But what should have amounted to a trip to HR somehow resulted in sales exceeding $40 million.

Then along comes Tony Horton with a reversal.

In the eighties, Horton was a struggling actor and aspiring comedian living in Los Angeles. To make ends meet, he did a bit of everything. He was a bartender, waiter, carpenter, handyman, and go-go dancer at Chippendales. As he pursued acting, Horton got seriously into working

8   Not Tim Hortons. That's a Canadian donut company.

out (e.g., weights, biking, runs, calisthenics, hitting the heavy bag), once helping a pal in the music industry lose more than twenty-five pounds.

Seeing results like that, Tom Petty (yes, *that* Tom Petty) asked Horton to help him get in shape four months before a tour. After Horton took Petty through his paces, Petty was so ripped that he started wearing his leather vest sans shirt on stage.

Suddenly, Horton was an in-demand celebrity trainer for Billy Idol, Bruce Springsteen, and Annie Lennox.

When Horton was approached by the company Beach Body to create a new fitness product, he used tactics that worked for his celebrity clients: "muscle confusion" (i.e., variety), a cheeky attitude, and of course, tough workouts six days a week. The high-intensity program features weight training, plyometrics, kickboxing, cardio, yoga, and the AbRipper. Not convinced? The company asks that you have your health assessed by a doctor before you begin.

You might know the workout as Power 90 Extreme (P90X).

P90X was invented with an inverted promise from other products in the market: P90X is hard. P90X is hard. P90X is hard. I know this to be true. While researching this story, I did a workout with Horton in his backyard and was sore for two and a half days. I didn't know my groin even had those muscles.

P90x flipped everything the industry was doing. A session can take ninety minutes. You won't see results in just ten days. It costs more. Yet the program sold over four million DVDs—and is worth $200 million to its parent company, Beach Body.

In addition to the sales, P90X became the most pirated DVD of the day—people were ripping how to get ripped. Bad joke. Where's Shane when I need him?

By reversing the status quo of exercise from as easy as possible to intentionally difficult, P90X tapped the market of underserved achievers. And, as Horton quipped, "The Shake Weight became a paperweight."

This is just one example of a reversal at work in business. Let's look closer at this principle through the eyes of comedy so you can begin designing reversals of your own.

ARCHITECTING A REVERSAL

Flipping what is expected in the mind of the audience is one of the first tricks—likely the first—a comedian learns.

The reversal can be seen in a comedy premise, such as a bit about bullies being good. A movie's plot can be based on a reversal. For example, in the movie *Trading Places*, a street hustler, Eddie Murphy, and a wealthy banker, Dan Akroyd...trade places.

The typical romantic comedy follows a standard storyline: Boy gets girl. Boy loses girl. Boy gets girl back. The movie *Trainwreck*, however, is a reverse rom-com. The leads switch stereotypical roles. Amy Schumer plays a party girl who resists monogamy until a kind, successful doctor (played by Bill Hader) helps her see the benefits of "settling down." Flipping the typical romantic comedy premise refreshed an otherwise tired storyline—and made $140 million at the box office.

A reversal can also occur as part of a punchline. Stand-up comedians will often set up an expectation at the beginning of a joke, only to reverse course at the end.

Chuck Roy is a six-foot-three, two-hundred-and-seventy-pound bear of a comedian. He is also a reversal personified: a gay Republican. Here's his system for creating comedy reversals:

Step 1: Start with an anecdote or phrase. This is the setup.

Here's Chuck Roy's setup:

I'm from New Hampshire where the State Motto is, 'Live Free or Die'...

Identify the direction the anecdote or phrase takes the audience.

Step 2: Turn the anecdote or phrase. This will be your punchline.

To find the perfect punchline, Roy asks three questions:

- What is the reverse of that direction?
- What is the opposite idea of the phrase?
- Is there a switcheroo?

I'm from New Hampshire where the State Motto is, 'Live Free or Die'. **I chose move.**

Step 3: Pause for the laugh.

I added this one.

Roy is still young. Here's another example from one of the masters, Henny "The King of the One Liner" Youngman:

When I read about the dangers of drinking...

And now Youngman's switcheroo:

*When I read about the dangers of drinking, **I gave up reading.***

Classic.

Enjoy these other comedy reversals:

> I tried being a stay-at-home mom for eight weeks. I liked
> the stay-at-home part. Not too crazy about the mom part.
>
> —ALI WONG

> My sister was with two men in one night. She could hardly
> walk after that. Can you imagine? Two dinners!
>
> —SARAH SILVERMAN

> My parents were strict. My mom and dad once made me
> smoke an entire pack of cigarettes. An entire pack of cig-
> arettes in one sitting...just to teach me a valuable lesson...
> about brand loyalty.
>
> —ANTHONY JESELNIK

Reversals are a common part of a good roast. While hosting the Golden Globes, Tina Fey and Amy Poehler used
a reversal to cleverly poke fun at George Clooney's Lifetime Achievement Award:

> George Clooney married Amal Alamuddin this year. Amal
> is a human rights lawyer who worked on the Enron case,
> was an adviser to Kofi Annan regarding Syria, and was

selected for a three-person UN commission investigating rules of war violations in the Gaza Strip. So tonight, *her husband* is getting a lifetime achievement award.

DIVERGENT THINKING

Reversals challenge the accepted way of thinking, and thinking in new ways is essential for creativity.

Creativity occurs when you find an appropriate, original solution to a problem. That is, you successfully solve a problem in a new way. Reversals don't always help find an appropriate solution, but when they do, it is typically original.

Some problems don't require creativity, because they only have one answer. Math problems are typically structured that way (e.g., 2+2 = ___), as well as most standardized tests. There is a single solution to be systematically discovered. Those problems require convergent thinking (something that AI does quite well, by the way).

When there is more than one possible solution, the problem requires what is called divergent thinking—the ability to take an idea in multiple directions.

The Alternative Uses Test is one way that scientists measure people's creative ability. An everyday item is placed in front of a person—a brick, nail file, or paper-clip. The person is given a couple of minutes to come up with as many "alternative" uses as possible. For example, a paperclip could be used as an ink pen or nose ring. The results are measured along four dimensions: 1) the number of alternatives, 2) their originality, 3) the range of ideas, and 4) how detailed the thought is.

A research study found that one's ability to be funny is positively correlated with performance on the Alternative Uses Test. Moreover, comedians are so good at creative thinking that an MIT study that featured a brainstorming competition between professional product designers and improvisational comedians revealed that the comedians' ideas were 25 percent more creative.[9]

Reversals help encourage divergent thinking and thus are useful for business. Generating an opposing perspective facilitates additional solutions that are not naturally considered.

BUSINESS REVERSALS

Let's look at some examples of how the world of business

9   Kudrowitz, B. (2010). "Haha and Aha! : Creativity, Idea Generation, Improvisational Humor, and Product Design" (PhD diss., Massachusetts Institute of Technology).

applies the concept of reversals to attack the status quo and find a seriously creative solution.

Get Stupid

Imagine trying to compete with Apple and Samsung in the smartphone market. If everyone is going smart, reverse course and go...dumb. That's what Brooklyn-based entrepreneurs Joe Hollier and Kaiwei Tang did by inventing the Light Phone 2, aka the "dumb phone."

The phone does the basics: text messaging, calls, alarm, and simple directions. It satisfies people's desire to be less connected to the digital world and present in the real world. I called Tang on his dumb phone, and he told me, "People don't need to carry a mini computer to the farmers' market."

The Light Phone 2 earned five times its goal on the crowdfunding site Indiegogo. Looks like your dad's old flip phone is back in style. Now be a good kid and help him set the clock on his VCR.

Down to _____

When it comes to dating, there are two predominant perspectives: people who want love and people who want lust.

Dating apps were founded on targeting the former—those looking for love in long-term committed relationships. They evolved from the likes of Match.com and eHarmony. com to more targeted demographics like Christianmingle. com, Farmersonly.com, and Glutenfreesingles.com.

But the dating app OkCupid had a different idea. The company decided that coupling people up makes their app useless, so rather than focusing on "Finding Your Forever" the app targets "Finding Your For-Now." This reversal is their differentiator.

Their marketing actively celebrates how great it is to be single, even giving the acronym DTF (i.e., down to f*ck) a positive spin.

- Down to Floss Together
- Down to Focus on My Chakras
- Down to Furiously Make Out

Sure, my results from OkCupid have been so-so, but according to the company's CMO, the campaign resulted in a 50 percent boost in buzz for OkCupid.[10]

---

10 BTW, I'm looking to connect with someone who is *Down to Finance* my next book.

Don't Buy

On Black Friday 2011, Patagonia bought a full-page advertisement in the *New York Times* with an atypical message.

The status quo in advertising is to convince consumers to buy a product (e.g., "Limited time only") and build positive brand associations (e.g., "Better ingredients. Better pizza."). Advertisements typically avoid negative information about the company (e.g., "Our founder is a racist.").

But reversing course in advertising—whether to acknowledge negative elements of the product or even convince customers not to buy a product—has counterintuitive benefits.

The entire outdoor industry is talking about sustainability, but Patagonia walks the talk. The "DON'T BUY THIS JACKET" campaign asks consumers to consider purchasing only things they really need. The ad points out the environmental damage of producing the jacket—helping to build an authentic brand that is focused on decreasing the company's footprint on the environment. Ironically, during the time the campaign was running, the company saw sales increase nearly 34 percent.

And remember, DON'T TELL ANYONE YOU ARE ENJOYING THIS BOOK.

BUGS INTO FEATURES

There is a specific kind of reversal that is effective in both comedy and business: flipping a weakness into a strength. This reversal is different from the Patagonia jacket—they created a negative to gain attention. Turning a bug into a feature is about taking something that is actually negative (or perceived as negative) and turning it into an asset.

Comedians are constantly turning their bugs into features. They joke about being too fat, too skinny, too short, too tall, too hairy, or too bald. These kinds of self-deprecating jokes usually kick off a comedy set.

By making fun of the peculiar thing that the audience is already thinking about, the comedian creates a benign violation, breaks tension, increases sympathy, and most importantly, gives the comedian license to make fun of everything else.

SHTICK FROM SHANE

Comics often put their worst foot forward and then make fun of their foot until you like it. When I started doing stand-up, I was probably one of the shyest people to ever try it. Instead of masking my shyness, I used my timid Midwestern "aw shucks" disposition to deliver my darkest material in a forgivable and naïve way. Those violations become more benign.

A THIRD MIC

Neal Brennan is the funniest person you've yet to hear of. I met Brennan many years ago at the Just for Laughs Comedy Festival in Montreal. I recognized him from playing a background character in a sketch for *Chappelle's Show.*

At the time, I didn't know that Brennan co-created *Chappelle's Show.* Don't let the name of the show fool you. Without Brennan, there is no *Chappelle's Show*. He helped write some of the most famous sketches: Racial Draft, Mad Real World, and Frontline—Clayton Bigsby.[11]

After the show ended, Brennan got serious about stand-up comedy, but he struggled to make it big. He is a nice guy—super generous, actually—but Neal lacks the warmth that helps an audience connect to a stand-up comedian.

Put yourself in Brennan's shoes: you write great jokes, but you can't become a great stand-up comedian because you lack the natural likeability that your friends Dave Chappelle and Chris Rock have on stage. What do you do?

Brennan decided to turn his bug into a feature in his Netflix comedy special *3 Mics*. In the show, he switches between three microphone stands, alternating between "One-liners," "Stand Up," and "Emotional Stuff." That third mic is the best part of the show, where he takes all of the things that made him less likable and speaks authentically about them. He discusses his struggles with depression and reflects on an abusive relationship with his father.

Brennan's performance was so compelling that *3 Mics* received better reviews than Chris Rock's special *Tambourine*.

---

11 It is in the Clayton Bigsby video that Brennan appears. Look for the guy whose head explodes.

BUSINESS BUGS

The concept of turning bugs into features works as effectively in the business world as it does in comedy. This is most evident in computer programming. For example, the creator of the video game *Space Invaders* decided not to repair a glitch in the program that caused the invaders to speed up. The bug became an important feature: the game becomes more challenging the longer you play. Here are three more business bugs reframed as features.

Undo Send

In 2015, Google's engineers had a problem. Gmail messages were taking an unusually long time to send. The engineering team decided to turn the delay into a valuable opportunity for customers who have made a regrettable choice. The team turned the bug into a feature and introduced "undo send."

I wish my phone had this feature to undo autocorrect errors. When the duck is that coming out?

Wax and Waste

In 1969, the California Cedar Products company (Cal-Cedar) was producing wood slats for four million pencils per day. The process creates a lot of leftover sawdust. Rather than throw out all that sawdust, the company figured out that, when combined with petroleum wax, the sawdust could be used to create a starter log for the fireplace—Duraflame.

Eight years later, CalCedar's sales had increased from $7 million a year to $50 million a year—with half of those sales due to Duraflame.

Not New. Not Improved.

In the 1980s, Buckley's cough syrup was stuck at number nine in Canada's cough syrup market. In other words, the brand was in trouble. You see, Buckley's tasted awful.

The obvious solution was to eliminate the weakness. The company could have added a cherry flavor or changed its formula. Instead, the brand launched a campaign turning a bug (its awful taste) into a feature (a reason to believe the cough syrup works).

It tastes awful. And it works.

Implication: it works *because* it tastes awful.

The decision allowed the company to create a bunch of fun print ads, too:

"People swear by it. And at it."

"Our largest bottle is 200 ml. Anything more would be cruel."

By appealing to people's motivation to murder the virus in their body and the belief that real medicine shouldn't taste good, Buckley's eventually became the number-one cough syrup on the market. The company's repositioning was so effective that Buckley's spent only a quarter as much on advertising as some of its competitors. The success prompted pharma company Novartis to buy Buckley's in 2002.

IMPLICATION: SH*TSTORMING

Everyone knows the first rule of brainstorming: don't criticize ideas. Even with that rule in place, brainstormers are reluctant to share ideas. As a B-school professor, this makes me sad—because it is the truly outrageous stuff that has the potential for a profound insight.

Based on insights from the reversal, I invented a brainstorming hack that I call "Sh*tstorming."[12] When I run ideation workshops, I ask participants to create as many truly awful ideas as they can in an allotted amount of time.

Generating a sh*tstorm does three things for a group:

First, it overcomes the problem of criticizing ideas. The ideas are supposed to suck, so what is there to criticize?

Second, sh*tstorming is a lot of fun and serves as a good warm-up for a traditional brainstorming task.

Third, a sh*tstorm can lead to creative ideas that you normally wouldn't think of in traditional brainstorming. For instance, someone may say, "That idea is so crazy, it just might work." Or, after looking at the terrible ideas, you reverse them as well, and see if any of the bad ideas can become good.

The reversal is just one tool in the comedian's repertoire and is part of a larger skill set we can apply to business: the ability to step out of the (main)stream.

You can download a sh*tstorming exercise as part of the *Shtick to Business* workbook at PeterMcGraw.org.

---

12 Or the HR-friendly name "Shtickstorming."

SHTICK FROM SHANE

Hey, Pete, how's this for a sh*tstorm?

What if you added commentary from a comic that no one has ever heard of?

Shane, that's so crazy, it just might work.

DEVELOP YOUR SHTICK

A good reversal in comedy can reap huge payoffs—better premises, plots, and punchlines. In business, as in comedy, we can only achieve the payoff when we let go of the status quo.

In the world of business and beyond, you might find enacting the reversal to be challenging. You should expect resistance because you are likely thinking differently than others. You don't have to tell people what you are doing in the background. All that matters is the quality of the solutions to your problems.

Choose a problem you are facing and start producing an opposing perspective.

- If you are struggling with how to lower costs, you could ask, "How can we increase costs instead? What benefit would that bring us? Could it actually create more value?"

- If you are tasked with figuring out how to attract more customers, you could instead ask, "Are there costly customers that we can fire?"
- At the same time you are considering lowering your prices, you could think, "How might I raise prices?"
- If your marketing communications say the same thing as your competitors, you could ask, "How might we say the opposite?"
- When you are lamenting your weakness, try asking "How might I see this weakness as a strength?"
- Thinking of putting this book down? Do a switcharoo and read the whole thing and tell everyone you know to do the same.

I've included a template for this kind of thinking in the *Shtick to Business* workbook on my website.

Now that you're well-versed in reversals, let's add a layer. Coming to the stage is your first Act Out, all about the power of three.

ACT OUT: NOT ONE.
NOT TWO. THREE.

Nikki Glaser is the ideal comedian to invite to a Comedy Central Roast. She's smart, fearless, and, as you will later learn, has a foolproof process for dropping comedy bombs on Alec Baldwin, Bruce Willis, and Justin Beiber.

At a recent show, she used a reversal to take down Martha Stewart:

> "My mom learned everything from Martha Stewart. Cooking and cleaning and withholding affection."

As Glaser's crack reveals, the reversal can complement another comedy 101 tactic: The Rule of Three. Comedians often set up a pattern, and then break it in an amusing way.

Indeed, good things seem to come in threes. (Allegedly, so do bad things.) There is a completeness to the number three. A three-act structure is the norm in theater and movies. Papers and presentations have three parts: introduction, body, and conclusion. And of course there's always the helpful reminder to, "stop, drop, *and* roll."

The same rule applies to business slogans, which tend to have three words or the cadence in a set of three:

- Just Do It
- I'm Lovin' It
- Snap Crackle Pop

Psychology and marketing studies on persuasion find that two arguments are too few, but four is often too many (at least when the audience knows that a message is meant to persuade).

So the next time you ask for a raise, give three compelling reasons. If you only have two, wait till you have three.

SHTICK FROM SHANE

I often use the rule of three. First, I set up the premise. Second, I build an expectation. Third, I talk about my genitals.

CHAPTER 2

STEP OUT OF
THE STREAM

Comedy requires courage—courage to do things that have never been done and say things that have never been said.

Hannah Gadsby is courageous.

She opens her Netflix comedy special *Nanette* by discussing her discomfort living in a small rural town in Australia. Gadsby grew up in Smithton, Tasmania (pop. 3,818), which she loved but had to leave "when I found out I was a little bit lesbian."

You see, homosexuality was a crime in Tasmania until 1997.

Gadsby makes self-deprecating jokes about being a lesbian and living in a place that was so hostile to her orientation. She didn't have access to information about being gay, and the info she had access to was mostly about gay men:

> For a long time, I knew more facts about unicorns than I did lesbians.
>
> (Pause)
>
> There are no facts about unicorns.

Comedy gold.

As the special goes on, she shares that there is something she's been considering quite seriously: quitting comedy.

> For the past year I've been questioning it. Reassessing. I think it's healthy for an adult human to take stock, pause, and reassess. When I first started doing 'the comedy' over a decade ago, my favorite comedian was Bill Cosby. There you go. It's very healthy to reassess, isn't it?
>
> I built a career out of self-deprecating humor. That's what I've built my career on. I don't want to do that anymore.
>
> Because do you understand what self-deprecation means

when it comes from somebody who already exists in the margins? It's not humility. It's humiliation. I put myself down in order to speak, in order to seek permission to speak. I simply will not do that anymore. Not to myself or anybody who identifies with me.

She goes on to say that in order to make her jokes land, she's had to omit much of the truth—the trauma she's faced as a woman and a lesbian in a world that's not always welcoming to women and lesbians. She then tells the whole truth about being sexually abused as a child, physically assaulted at seventeen, and raped in her twenties.

Hannah Gadsby breaks the rules of a stand-up special. Her audience comes for a comedy show and instead receives the decidedly unfunny life experience of a marginalized woman.

She closes to a standing ovation.

What can we learn from Gadsby? First, it takes an upside-down comedic perspective to recognize that her livelihood might actually be making her worse off. Second, she took a different approach to a traditional comedy set. This is reminiscent of Neal Brennan's 3 Mics where he omits jokes for a third of his show. Gadsby goes further, undoing the benign violations that she created at the beginning of the show and laying bare the violations that form the basis for the jokes.

This kind of courage can lead to great rewards.

Since her attempt to quit comedy, Hannah Gadsby is working more than ever—forging her own path.

BOLDLY GO

I suggest you mimic comedians and look to step out of the *mainstream*. You know the clichés...go against the grain, zig when others zag, think outside the box. (Ugh...I promised myself that I would think of an outside the box way of saying outside the box.)

Comedians aren't good rule followers. They're usually not the kind of people you want leading a boardroom, classroom, or newsroom (unless that newsroom is *The Daily Show*). But not following rules is a key to success in comedy. By their own nature and by the nature of their work, comedians must think differently than everyday people—and hence they act differently than everyday people.

To step out, comedians must first observe the world around them and see the way things truly are—the way others are thinking and behaving. From here, they can take actions that violate the status quo.

Comedy often begins from stepping out, in thought and deed, so much so that this could have (should have?) been chapter one. "Reverse it" is a special case of stepping out of the stream.

But comedy is more than just creating a benign violation—it's creating a benign violation that no one has ever seen or heard before. Comedy requires novelty. And let's face it—it's hard to do something that has never been done before.

Because of this premium placed on novelty, not only do comedians have to break the rules of the status quo in the normal world, but they must do it differently than the comedians who broke the rules before them.

Similarly, great business opportunities are often novel, and yet too many businesses focus on imitation, thinking that it's going to lead to success. But if the goal of business is to be the best, then it helps to do something different, something that is new. Solve a problem that has never been solved or solve the problem in a way it has never been solved.

Thinking and acting like a comedian will help you recognize the rules, question if the rules are any good, and then break them to your benefit.

SHTICK FROM SHANE

I started doing comedy in Boston, a city that has a rich comedian history. Early on in my career, I was exceptionally dry and monotone. Once someone compared me to the Boston great Steven Wright, and I was flattered. I learned the value of being different early on in my career from him. Not only was Steven one of the very first comics I really liked as a kid, but he also had an inspiring rise in the business built on a freight train of one-liners:

- "You can't have everything. Where would you put it?"
- "I've written several children's books...Not on purpose."
- "I stayed up one night playing poker with Tarot cards. I got a full house and four people died."

Steven started comedy during the Boston comedy boom. Clubs were popping up everywhere, every show was selling out, and people were flooding into the business.

The scene quickly got filled with a bunch of Boston meathead hacks who thought they were kings because they killed in front of a bunch of drunk, rowdy audiences with boorish material. Steven was different. He looked odd, sounded odder, and he was as cerebral as he was weird. He was an outcast.

One day Johnny Carson's booker came through town and all the meatheads showcased for him. Back then, if you got picked to perform on Carson, you had a career. If you got invited to Carson's couch after your set, you had a big career.

This was their big shot. To their surprise, not only was Steven Wright on the showcase, but he was the only one the booker picked to be on Carson. The booker had never seen anyone like Wright, and something happened that had never happened before—he was invited back on the show just five days later.

He was new—and different. Soon after, he became one of the biggest comics of his generation.

SEE THE RULE. BREAK THE RULE.

Comedians are like anthropologists, with three exceptions. First, they write jokes instead of peer-reviewed journal articles. Second, they live within the culture they are observing. Third, they try to sleep with the people they're studying.

Yet both comedians and anthropologists are seeking the truth. The ability to observe and dissect the behaviors of a culture is a gift.

Comedians are able to see through the BS and make novel insights about their own culture because, although they live in it, they never quite fit into it. The price of a comedian's life—never quite fitting in—is also the gift.

Chris Rock's popularity with both black and white audiences occurs because he understands both worlds. This is in large part because he was never quite comfortable in either world. He jokes that the neighborhood where he grew up in Brooklyn was so bad that the McDonald's went out of business. Yet he was too much of a nerd to fit in there. He was bussed to a white school, where he felt just as much like an outsider.

Comedians exist in what's called a "liminal space." John Wenzel, a journalist who covers comedy explained it like this to me, "Comedians are liminal workers. It gives them power."

A liminal space can be physical—a transition from one place to another (doorways, for example, are liminal). A liminal space can also be psychological, such as the mindset of a person in a life transition. If you're graduating from school you're in a liminal space. You're no longer a student, but you're not a professional. Engaged. Pregnant. Newly retired. And so on. Ceremonies are often associated with liminality (if that is not already a word, it is now).[13]

In a psychological context, liminal space refers to the fact that what you're going through is temporary. You're not rooted in anything familiar. As a result, you experience a shift in perspective and identity.

Comedians *live* in liminal spaces because they never quite belong. This allows them to separate from the world around them in order to observe it.

A liminal mindset also helps comedians to leave *ideas* behind. This enables them to create novelty by constantly pushing forward, both by challenging themselves and by escaping the competition.

---

13 Since learning the concept, my students keep telling me that their homework is in a liminal space.

FISH OUT OF WATER

There is a rich history of observational comedians who make jokes about the way things are: the weird, strange, ridiculous, exasperating world right in front of our own eyes. But we don't see it. We need comedy to see it.

Jerry Seinfeld, the quintessential observational comedian, says that comedians aren't human, but they're not aliens either. They're humanoids. Close enough to fit in, but different enough to make objective observations.

As an example, consider Seinfeld's bit about dogs and their owners:

> On my block, a lot of people walk their dogs. And I always see them walking along with their little poop bags, which to me is just the lowest function of human life. If aliens are watching this through telescopes, they're going to think the dogs are the leaders. If you see two life forms, one of them is making a poop, the other one's carrying it for him, who would you assume is in charge?

Seinfeld is the exemplar of the anthropologist, of the comedian as humanoid. It's not just that great comedians tend not to fit into the culture around them. They intentionally seek not to.

Sebastian Maniscalco is another observational comedian

who is on the ascent. He's a modern-day Seinfeld with bits on airport check-ins, shopping, and his grandmother living in the basement. For example:

> I was sitting in my house a couple of weeks ago, just relaxing. My doorbell rang. This is weird. It's a different feeling when your doorbell rings today as opposed to twenty years ago, right? Twenty years ago, your doorbell rang, that was a happy moment in your house. It's called "company." You'd be sitting there on a Thursday night watching TV. Your doorbell rang, the whole family shot off the couch. "Oh my God! Put the lights on, somebody's here! We got people!"

> The whole family went to the door. The kids were in socks, they slid up to the door. Nobody looked to see who it was. You just opened up the door and you were like, "Oh my God, look at them. Look at this here." And you'd ask them, "What the hell are you doing here?" And the person would be like, "I was in the neighborhood. I thought I might stop by, see how the kids are doing." You're like, "Oh, come on in. We're going to have some cake."

> But now, your doorbell rings? It's like, "What the f*ck?"

> "Get down, Ma! Army crawl! Army crawl, get in the closet. Go get the sword in the living room. Somebody get the sword underneath the couch in the living room, there's a sword."

What makes Maniscalco different from other observational comedians is the high level of physicality he brings to the stage. He is dressed up but energetically acts out the above bit—jumping out of a couch, sliding up to the front door as if he was in socks, and frantically orchestrating his mom to army crawl.[14]

It takes an outsider's perspective to see the absurdity most of us are immersed in and simply accept. For example, what would you say is the most complicated word in the English language? According to the Finnish comedian, Ismo, it's "ass":

> There are so many meanings with the word ass. I think it's the most complicated word in English. I've been trying to write a whole dictionary about just ass. Like for example a lazy ass. That means lazy. Like, "My lazy ass husband." It's the same sentence without the ass...And long ass means long, like a long ass flight. It's a long flight. My definite favorite one, a grown ass man. It turns out it means a grown man. The entire man has grown, not only his ass.

---

14 As an aside, I have an example of why Sebastian Maniscalco is a comedian and I'm not. He has a joke about men who wear flip flops, "When did it become appropriate to come out in a flip-flop sandals for a steak dinner? I'm trying to enjoy a T-Bone, and I gotta look at some guy's hoof."

Independently, I had made a similar observation. I once proudly tweeted, "When a middle-aged man wears flip-flops, he's choosing his own comfort over the comfort of others."

You, dear reader, can decide which one is funnier. But I'm still proud of mine.

This is way better on stage. Check out the video on my YouTube channel.

SHTICK FROM SHANE

I travel full time. Usually three cities a week. I dine out by myself nearly every single day and rarely talk to anybody. To the average person, this sounds lonely.

It's one of my favorite things to do in life.

Why? I get to watch people. I get to listen to them.

The average person thinks that being a fly on the wall is a voyeuristic adventure to eavesdrop on people's deepest, darkest secrets. It's not. It's boring. Most people are boring most of the time, and their dinnertime topics follow suit...on the surface.

But those with an outsider's insight, like comics, can see below the surface. They notice the underlying secrets—symptoms of the human condition that unceasingly spring to the surface.

I can look at a group getting together and know whether they are family or having a business meeting. In a family I understand their relationships to one another and how long it's been since they last got together. In a business meeting I can spot the hierarchy of everyone at the table—the top down of the food chain. I know when a couple is a one-night stand or a long relationship that has gone stale.

The words people are saying are rarely what they're actually saying. It takes a long time to see this. And what it reveals is a new point of view. This is precisely why a comic's observational joke about a very common situation is funny. They have a fresh look on what everyone else has seen a thousand times. Comics are alien anthropologists.

THERMOMETER OR THERMOSTAT

The majority of a comedian's power is in observation—their ability to take the temperature of an individual, room, or even an entire culture. They act like a thermometer, measuring what is happening and making it known to others.

Doug Stanhope, who you will get to know in chapter three, is a caustic stand-up who has a bit that identifies how much comedy points things out but doesn't make change:

> I said, I don't care anymore. I used to have some type of social relevance in my act and there was a point where I really gave a sh*t about stuff, to a point where it was ruining my life. And I guess ten years ago I thought, well, I'm going to change the world...

> But the whole changing the world thing never really kicked in.

> The revolution was starting where I thought I could yell at 200 people in a bar every night and change the world. Yeah, didn't quite happen like Egypt and Syria. No. And it's frustrating because you do a bit and then you go, oh, that's really good...And then it just appears, the problem is still there and someone will say, "oh, abortion's back in the news," and you go, why? I already solved that on a 2004 release. How could it possibly still exist? I've yelled at thousands of drunk people about that.

Based on the time I have spent with comedians, I'm not surprised Stanhope's tirades didn't kick off waves of change. Overwhelmingly, comedians are going to choose laughs over changing the world anyway. But on occasion you get a comedian whose observations do more than take the temperature—they *change* the temperature. They shift from thermometer to thermostat.

One of the earliest examples of thermostat comedy is Lenny Bruce. He was arrested multiple times in the early 1960s for obscenity—specifically for saying a word that rhymes with sockcucker. These kinds of charges were often dismissed, but Bruce went to trial and was convicted of obscenity in 1964, along with club owner Howard Solomon. Lenny Bruce was later pardoned after his death. His commitment to free speech helped loosen up obscenities laws. George Carlin continued his fight with his bit about *Seven Dirty Words You Can't Say on Television.*

Another comedian who radically changed the temperature of the room is Hannibal Buress. He started doing comedy in 2002 as a stand-up and a writer; you may have seen Buress playing himself on *The Eric Andre Show.*

Hannibal Buress has a "bug into feature" joke about how his name hurts his dating life—a few too many potential partners are reminded of *Silence of the Lambs* villain,

Hannibal Lecter. Not a name you want called out at the moment of climax.

He worked as a writer for *SNL* for a couple years but left having had only one of his sketches aired. No one was calling out his name in the writer's room either...

In 2014, Buress went onstage and talked about how annoyed he is by Bill Cosby's smugness—telling young Black men to "pull up their pants":

> 'I (Bill Cosby) can talk down to you because I had a successful sitcom.' Yeah, but you rape women, Bill Cosby, so turn the crazy down a couple notches.

> 'I don't curse on stage!' but you're a rapist so...

> That sh*t is upsetting, if you didn't know about it, trust me. When you leave here, Google 'Bill Cosby rape.' It ain't funny. That sh*t has more results than Hannibal Buress.

Other comedians—Tina Fey, Amy Poehler, Tracy Morgan—had referred to the allegations over the year. Burress had been working on the bit for about six months. Then, in 2014, *Philadelphia Magazine* posted a poor-quality video of the joke, and things—as the kids used to say—went kray.

Buress's courage to critique Cosby's hypocrisy, openly

questioning why nothing had been done about this open secret, was a catalyst for Cosby's victims coming forward. The joke spurred an awareness and an investigation.

That's a thermostat.

SEEING AN OPPORTUNITY

Switching away from comedy, I believe that businesses can learn a valuable lesson from emulating humanoids and the way they see the world.

At times, the best innovations are so simple and so obvious that people wonder why someone didn't make it happen sooner. Entrepreneurial success often comes from an uncanny ability—which comedians have honed so well—to see the world differently.

Once you see the gap between have and need, you can make courageous choices to make it happen.

Closet in the Cloud

While they were classmates at Harvard Business School, Jennifer Hyman and Jennifer Fleiss would regularly meet for lunch to discuss business ventures.

At the time, the platform economy was on the upswing.

Many successful companies simply connect consumers to solutions: Task Rabbit, Lyft, and of course, Tinder, Bumble, Ok Cupid, Grindr, etc. Be a middleman and take a cut.

The idea for Hyman and Fleiss's venture was born when Hyman's sister Becky bought a dress that cost more than her rent. Why? She *needed* that dress.

Turns out, many women had a workaround when they needed a special dress for a special occasion—and needed to avoid credit card debt. These women would buy an expensive dress from a fancy department store such as Neiman Marcus, Saks 5th Avenue, or Nordstrom's. They then would leave the tags on, tuck the tags in, wear the dress, and pray to the party gods they didn't spill their red wine. Then after the event, they'd return it to the store. The practice earned the euphemism, "wardrobing."

Hyman and Fleiss believed that if women had a reasonable alternative, they could act with more integrity. So the partners created an e-commerce site, Rent the Runway, which allows customers to borrow highly fashionable dresses for about 20 percent of the retail price. The dress is rented, worn, returned, dry cleaned, and rented to other customers.

By shining a light in the shadows—people who buy and

return high-end items—Hyman and Fleiss landed on an out-of-the-stream solution where everyone wins. On launch day, the *New York Times* published an article about Rent the Runway and 100,000 new customers signed up for the service. The founders met their first-year sales goal in three weeks.

Concrete Dreams

In Mexico, concrete homes are the norm. Not only an ideal match for the warm climate, concrete is relatively inexpensive and easy to DIY. An addition is a great option for families who need extra space.

Still, most low-income families live in homes that are small and overcrowded, despite owning their land and having access to affordable building materials. They forgo building the much-needed addition to their home.

The reason? A generous and celebratory culture.

Rather than using extra money to build an addition to their home, Mexican families are more likely to use it toward gifts and celebrations—everything from weddings to baptisms to quinceañeras. And so families who need additional space to thrive become stuck in a cycle from which they can't and won't break free. Those who do build an addition often take seven long years to make it happen.

Culture is a hard thing to change.

Enter the Mexican company Cemex, which sells cement and concrete.[15] Rather than fight against the culture that puts off home renovations in favor of giving to others, they wove their product into the existing culture, making it more available to those who need it. How did they do it?

They set up a program that allowed families to pay into a fund that helped others purchase building materials for their homes.

The program, *Patrimonio Hoy*, is based on the existing cultural practice of *tanda*—a group of people who pull a portion of funds together and then give the "pot" to one person in the group at a time. Money is collected regularly until each person in the group has taken their turn winning the pot.

Families in the program can save for building materials for their own additions and help others at the same time. This shifts the function of saving for an addition from a practical choice to an emotional one—one that fulfills the cultural needs of the people it serves.

By recognizing this status quo, Cemex was able to

---

15   There is a difference between concrete and cement. Cement is an ingredient in concrete. Take that to your next cocktail party conversation.

align and leverage it for the good of all. And business is booming.

A Toasty Deal

My executive MBA students, many of whom are already in executive positions, often ask me, "What should I do when X happens?" or "How do I deal with Y challenge?" They are disappointed when I tell them that I won't tell them what to do, but I will tell them how to approach the problem. Find the insight.

"Find the insight!" I yell at the class. I don't really yell, but you get the picture.

TurboChef is an example of a company who needed an insight. They sell a convection oven—a magnificent technology—that heats up food fast. It's like a microwave without the sogginess. At $4,000 a pop, however, the oven was too expensive to sell to everyday people.

TurboChef needed a different customer—one who needed a better way to heat things quickly but who could also afford such an expensive oven. In 2004, they found someone: Subway.

At the time, Subway was facing competition from Quiznos. Along with their delectable pepper bar,

Quiznos would heat your sandwich into a toasty tasty treat.

The problem with TurboChef's plan was convincing Subway to pay $80 million dollars to put the oven in every store—especially if that cost got passed on to franchisees.

Though it seemed as if melted cheese and warm meat was never to be, TurboChef's out-of-the-stream insight created a triple win.

At the time, Pepsi held the beverage contract for all Subway franchises. (Can you see where this is going?) The oven company approached Coca-Cola with an idea: what if *they* purchased the ovens for Subway, and in exchange Subway switched their beverage contract from Pepsi to Coke?

Rather than fighting a potentially unwinnable uphill battle by going at Subway directly, the convection oven company looked with fresh eyes and saw the possibilities. Now everyone was better off.

Well, except for Pepsi.[16]

---

16 That said, I am willing to drink Pepsi in order to fund my next book project *Shtick to Retirement: What the Masters of Comedy can Teach You about Caribbean Vacations, Sleeping in Hammocks, and Curing Hangovers.*

TAKING RISKS

Once you can recognize the rules, you are closer to stepping out of the stream. But to truly get there—to break the rules—you must be willing to take a risk.

As humans, we are wired to avoid risk: to play nice, follow rules, and get along. This traces back to our hunter-gatherer days when we lived in very small tribal communities and it was vitally important to fit in. If you didn't fit in, you'd get left behind. And if you were left behind, you'd starve.

Life was simpler back then.

Nowadays, there are costs if you get left behind: spend time downloading Uber Eats and spend money tipping the driver.

Nevertheless, our tribal instincts tell us to *get along or else*. It is emotionally painful to be left behind, and that keeps us from taking chances.

Thankfully, there's a segment of the tribe that's not as risk-averse. They're the weirdos who see if this odd berry is edible. The crazy ones who track animals far into the wildlands. The ding dongs who are actually attracted to the idea of meeting a new band of people, not terrified by it. These are the people that help their tribe discover new foods, new territories, and new ideas. Sometimes, it leads to war. But hey, sometimes it works out for the better.

There is a reason why valedictorians rarely have commensurate success in business. While intelligent and hard-working, their disposition to follow the rules (and the *sure* path to modest success) has them sitting in the front of the class, excelling at standardized tests, dotting every I and crossing every T.

Class clowns misbehave. They don't play well in highly structured environments and they are not afraid to disappoint the teacher, because they have a different set of priorities. They aren't looking for the *sure* thing; they're looking for the *next great* thing. When needed, they will *create* and *become* the next great thing.

Great comedy and great business take the approach of the class clown by intentionally finding the rules they can bend and those they can break. And then stepping out to bend and break them.

This boldness comes with great risk, but also great rewards.

WORKING THEIR OWN WAY

Comedians don't like to do what they are told. And they

don't worry too much about their reputation either. This allows them to be highly creative and take risks. You don't need me to tell you that. I'm sure you have stories about your favorite comedians or comedy shows that you could tell me. Here are three that I like.

Ambiguously Bold

The stand-up comedy world is cutthroat. Getting good requires suffering nightly at a variety of open mics. For the average open mic, you arrive at the venue and put your name on the list, then wait patiently for your turn, forced to listen to a bunch of other comedians tell truly terrible jokes until you finally get your chance to go up for three minutes to tell your truly terrible jokes. Ideally, you want to do as many sets as you can in a single evening.

As a young comedian, Eric Marlon Bishop was competing for these spots. He'd arrive at the venue and put his name on the list. If you've been to one of these open mics, you know that the overwhelming majority of comedians are young men (especially when Bishop was starting out). Oftentimes, the bookers running the open mics wanted more variety in the line-up than dude after dude, so they might move the few women up the list to perform earlier.

When checking in one day, Bishop had a wicked idea. He didn't put *his* name on the list. Rather he put a name that sounded like a woman's name. In fact he put several names that sounded like a woman's name: Tracey Brown, Stacey Green, and...

Jamie Foxx.

Guess which name they called first? The rest, as they say, is history.

Saturday Night Death Match

Getting on *Saturday Night Live* is notoriously difficult. Producer and co-creator Lorne Michaels makes everything about the process challenging, even intimidating. In the show's forty-five-year history, only two cast members—Kristen Wiig and Dana Carvey—made it to air right away.

To break into *SNL*, comedians are willing to take a risk.

As a young comedian, Eddie Murphy called talent coordinator Neil Levy daily to beg for a chance—saying that he had eighteen siblings who were counting on him. To make him shut up, Levy agreed to use Murphy as an extra. But after the show's staff saw the screen test, Murphy was hired as a cast member. Note: Murphy has two brothers.[17]

---

17 One of them is Charlie Murphy, known for his hilarious *True Hollywood Stories* on *Chappelle's Show*. RIP Charlie.

Victoria Jackson auditioned for SNL, but Michaels didn't think she was up to snuff. So she decided to amp up her chances by using an appearance on *The Tonight Show with Johnny Carson* to impress Michaels. She told the audience her intention and proceeded to perform a variety of impressions (a staple of *SNL* auditions), challenging Carson to guess each one. It sealed the deal and she made it on the show as a cast member from 1986 to 1992.

Will Ferrell chickened out in his wild attempt to get on the show, but the story is still worth telling. Ferrell had a meeting with Michaels before his second audition. The plan was to bring a briefcase with $25,000 in counterfeit money. Ferrell was going to place it on the desk, say, "Money talks," and walk out the door. However, the meeting was too tense. Ferrell chickened out and felt foolish for carrying a briefcase to an audition.

Part Bruce Lee. Part Buster Keaton

Bruce Lee is an original badass.

He spearheaded not only the practice of martial arts by creating Jeet Kun Do, but dramatically changed the way that Asians were presented in American film, debunking the stereotype of the emasculated Asian male. His contributions to film and martial arts became the new standard for the modern-day action film star.

Now, most "badass" action stars, such as Jason Statham and Dwayne "The Rock" Johnson, have contractual limitations for how many times they get punched and kicked on camera (i.e., gotta protect your brand). They want to make sure they're handing out the pain and not taking a beat down.

But one martial artist-turned-actor decided to take a different approach. A riskier approach. He decided to take all the hits. And the kicks. And the falls. And the nut-shots.

Jackie Chan is a new kind of badass.

Chan realized that he was never going to eclipse Bruce Lee as a fighter. And so, rather than be like Lee—a serious martial artist—Chan decided to become an unserious martial artist. This is his brand.

Rather than limiting the number of hits he takes, he seeks to maximize them: punched, kicked, thrown, dropped, crushed, beaten, and battered—often for comedic effect. This intentional choice helped him find his sweet spot in the marketplace.

In 2019, at age sixty-five, he was the fifth highest paid actor on the Forbes list. He has been in over 150 movies.

And he does all his own stunts, which, let's be honest,

makes him funnier and more badass than Statham and The Rock combined.

SHTICK FROM SHANE

I have been going against the grain since I was a kid in rural Wisconsin. For example, the adults in my life told me I was supposed to care about three things: God, the Green Bay Packers, and the Green Bay Packers.

I don't know what was more confusing to me, a white man in the clouds or some green blobs moving around a cold field. Being a brat that God made me to be, one day I decided that I would root for whatever team was playing the Packers.

I was six.

Grown adults would be absolutely furious with me...a kid, because they couldn't figure out that a child was messing with them. I thought that was hilarious...Worth every wedgie. I was hooked, and I have been pushing buttons ever since.

In high school I purposely wore a 49ers jacket because it was one of the teams Wisconsinites hated the most, which meant I was begging to get my ass kicked. In hindsight, I should have worn a Vikings hat to pull it all together.

RISKY BUSINESS

The very nature of high failure rates in business suggests that you need to take more chances, not fewer. Business demands risk-taking—informed risks, but risks nonetheless.

The ability to not only see what is different, but then take action on it, is what gives comedians and companies their cutting edge. Nearly every entrepreneurial success story involves a bit of luck, but it also often involves someone doing something they "shouldn't"—taking a risk.

Bet on Black

I teach a Federal Express case study to my MBAs. FedEx, as we know it today, was built on a brilliant idea: don't treat packages like people. For example, packages don't care about redeye flights (i.e., FedEx would send packages overnight), packages don't care about connections (i.e., FedEx used a "hub and spoke" with Memphis as the hub), and packages don't throw temper tantrums when their flight is delayed.

The case is a great learning tool, yet tough to teach. First, the case requires a bunch of math, and the students don't realize how much math matters to marketers. Moreover, the case is set in the 1970s and thus also feels "old" to the students. The thing that makes it truly difficult to teach is that, in hindsight, the success of overnight shipping seems so obvious. Students know the conclusion that they should come to. FedEx appears destined for success. Yet business school cases often ignore the importance of luck.

In fact, FedEx was dollars away from failing, not because

the business wasn't a good idea, but because (say it with me) *business is hard.* Early on, the founder Fred Smith was down to his last $5,000 and did not have enough funds to pay the fuel bill needed to make upcoming shipments (that is the equivalent of $31,000 in today's dollars). This was after every other penny had been pinched—everything from uncashed paychecks to employees using their personal credit cards to pay for fuel.

So Fred Smith did the only thing he could think of: he went to Vegas. There he made a run on the blackjack table and transformed the company's final five grand into $27K, enough to keep them afloat for one more week.

The point here is that even the most brilliant ideas just might require taking a briefcase full of (real) cash to Vegas.

Renting the Guru

Jennifer Hyman and Jennifer Fleiss knew they had a novel business concept with Rent the Runway.

Yet a difficulty of a platform business is that two sides of the marketplace need to be populated. Task Rabbit will fail if it is unable to find customers to buy tasks or find "rabbits" to do the tasks. In Rent the Runway's case, designers were initially not that excited about the idea. Yet the site needed designer dresses.

Hyman and Fleiss cold-emailed the fashion designer (and icon) Diane von Furstenberg, and got a "Yes, see you tomorrow" response. The co-founders drove down from Boston the next day wearing their DVF dresses. The five-minute meeting extended to well over an hour.

They got a second meeting, but on the way to it, von Furstenberg's assistant called to inform the co-founders that the meeting was canceled because, basically, "She is no longer interested in the idea."

Hyman told the assistant that they were "just around the corner" and could just come by for a quick hello. Before the assistant could tell her again (even more firmly) that von Furstenberg wasn't interested, Hyman said, "We're cutting out. Hello? We're cutting out." And hung up.

The founders decided to show up anyway. Even if security threw them out, they would have a great story to tell their friends.

They sped down the highway, made their way to von Furstenberg's office, and were not thrown out. The meeting, which wasn't supposed to happen at all, turned into von Furstenberg sharing valuable business market insight as well as connections to other designers.

This strategy works well—at least until your dean buys you a new phone.

Ask Forgiveness

How many door-to-door fax machine salespeople go on to become billionaires?

I know of one.

Back in her sales days, Sara Blakely had a pair of nice white pants that would show lines from her underwear. Blakely's solution was to cut the feet off her "control top" pantyhose to smooth the look. Problem solved.

Turns out this was a problem experienced by countless other women. Blakely went on to produce an undergarment that compresses and smooths the butt and thighs. A great idea. But great ideas are no guarantee for success. For Blakely to become a billionaire, she had to take risks.

She called the product Spanx. Edgy and fun to say. Step one.[18]

---

18 Many comedians believe that "K" sounds are funnier than non-K sounds. Blakely used that belief when naming Spanx.

At the time, packaging for pantyhose was drab. Blakely wanted people to be *excited* about their purchase so she made the packaging bright red with an illustration of three stylish women of different ethnicities. Step two.

At launch, she asked friends and family to purchase the product when it was first in stores, and she mailed them checks to reimburse them for their purchases. She called up everyone she knew in the cities where the product was being launched. Even friends she hadn't spoken to since fourth grade. Step three.

She managed to get the product into Neiman Marcus, but Spanx was placed in the hosiery department, a part of the store Blakely knew her customer would not venture. To ensure her product got noticed, she snuck around the store, waited until no one was looking, and moved the display next to the cash register. Fortunately, the employees assumed that the decision had been approved by some higher-ups. Sales spiked. Step four.

Blakely has never relied on traditional advertising or taken investments. As a result, she is the sole owner of the company. Step five.

Not surprisingly, when she was just starting out in her career, Blakely worked as a stand-up comedian.

So far in this chapter, I've talked about recognizing rules and being willing to take a risk to break them. But there's another way to *step out of the stream*, a reversal of breaking rules: making rules.

LEVERAGE LIMITS

Freedom is a common war cry if you are a thirteenth-century Scottish warrior, but great comedy is built on a lack of freedom. Even though comedians regularly break rules, conversely, they also use rules to be more creative. In fact, the greater the constraints, oftentimes the greater the creativity.

The most commonly-accepted model of the creative process is called the "Geneplore" model by Finke, Ward, and Smith (scientists—not a law firm).[19] That is the name they gave the model. Talk about settling on a name too soon.[20]

As the name suggests, the creative process had two stages: 1) Generate: where options are developed, and 2) Explore: where options are built upon and evaluated. The model is useful for understanding opportunities and threats to creativity. For example, being scared of backlash during

---

19 Finke, R., Ward, T. B., & Smith, S. M. (1992). *Creative cognition: Theory, research, and applications*. MIT Press.

20 Shane is from Wisconsin and he tells me there is a worse name. Cheese curds. He says they are quite tasty. Obviously, none of us want to try something called a cheese curd, so we will have to take his word for it.

the "explore" part of the process can lead to people holding back and not suggesting a potentially useful idea.

A study by consumer behavior researchers Page Moreau and Darren Dahl demonstrates the value of constraints.[21] It experimentally reveals when constraints make people more creative. Participants were asked to design a children's toy out of a variety of shapes: a cylinder, a pyramid, a cube, a hook, etc. There were twenty shapes available. Moreau and Dahl randomly assigned participants to one of four conditions with increasing degrees of constraint:

1. Select any five shapes, and you can use as many as you want.
2. Here are five shapes (randomly selected from the twenty), and you can use as many as you want.
3. Select any five shapes, and you must use all five.
4. Here are five shapes (randomly selected from the twenty), and you must use all five.

After participants finished, three design professionals judged the creativity level of the toys. The most creative toys, it turns out, were those made under the final condition, the one which had the biggest constraint.

This is good news. Rather than trying to eliminate con-

---

21 Moreau, C.P. & Dahl, D. (2005). Designing the solution: The impact of constraints on consumers' creativity, *Journal of Consumer Research*, 32, 13-22.

straints (which we often feel we need for creativity), you should embrace them. From this place you may arrive at better ideas for solving problems.

Let's look at some specific ways comedians leverage constraints.

DON'T SAY THAT

Unpopular opinion: Censorship is good. More than once, limiting language has paved the way for stellar comedy careers.

Stern Language

Howard Stern is known for ragging on the FCC, but their attempts to limit his "indecent" speech boosted Stern's career. His battles over censorship helped catapult him to the #1 radio show in the American market. The Shock Jock's escapades with the FCC provided ongoing controversial content for (often) libertarian listeners to eat up. At one point, the station implemented a seven-second delay to help censor his fine-worthy content. Still, Stern accumulated 2.5 million dollars in fines from the FCC over the course of his career. He went on to be the self-proclaimed "King of All Media" and fueled the rise of satellite radio.

You Mae Speak Freely

Long before Howard Stern, Mae West had her own show-down with the FCC. West is most well-known for her career as a Hollywood star in the 1920s and '30s, starring in films with her sultry voice—a voice the FCC thought was so sexy it made mundane statements titillating.

Before becoming a Hollywood star and dealing with censorship in film, Mae West wrote plays. In 1926, she wrote the cutting-edge, controversial play *Sex*, which she also produced and directed. The play is about a prostitute looking to marry a wealthy man. The entire cast was arrested for "obscenity and corrupting the morals of youth." West was the primary target. She was found guilty and sentenced to serve time. She could have avoided jail time by paying a fine, but she wanted the publicity. So she went to jail for the week. She was released two days early for good behavior, which she later claimed was "the first time I ever got anything for good behavior."

In order to work around the censors, she became a master of the double entendre:

A hard man is good to find.

When I'm good, I'm very good. But when I'm bad I'm better.

West's rise as a humorist came from the censorship that she

had to deal with in radio, film, and television. She famously said, "I believe in censorship, I made a fortune out of it."

But censorship doesn't just come from the outside, it can also be self-imposed—a way some creatives forge their path out of the stream.

SELF-INFLICTED CONSTRAINTS

Imagine that you develop a blockbuster product. You launch it, it sells well, and then you decide to stop selling it—even though it still creates value for your customers.

Welcome to the world of stand-up comedy. After filming a comedy special, many comedians retire the material and start fresh. Then, over the course of the year, they build from zero minutes of material until they have a new hour. This differentiates comedians from musicians. Comedians can't do covers, and they don't tour with their "greatest hits" like The Rolling Stones.

Professionals are constantly imposing their own constraints on their comedy, forcing themselves to create new material and pushing the boundaries of their own novelty.

Squeaky Clean

Some comedians take their self-censorship further and

impose a constraint to work *clean*. No F-bombs, cursing, cussing, going *blue*. Whatever their opinion, professionals comedians agree that working clean is the most difficult constraint—even more than novelty.

There is a tendency to think of boundary-pushing comedy as made up of jokes that tackle most taboo topics. Yet, working clean creates a boundary that can't be crossed. These comedians who work clean and work it well end up as some of the biggest names because of their broad appeal:

> I saw an ad for a pill that stops headaches and migraines before they start. That's some good marketing right there.
>
> "Are you in any pain?"
>
> "No, not at all."
>
> "I'm going to give you something for that."
>
> ELLEN DEGENERES[22]

My eye doctor told me this. I'm not making this up. He goes, "You know you have one eye set a little bit higher than your other eye?"

---

22 Ellen DeGeneres, the queen of clean, dropped an F-bomb in her 2019 Netflix comedy special, *Relatable*. The punchline to the world's longest setup.

"No, I didn't know that."

He goes, "It's no big deal. It doesn't affect your vision or anything. I just thought you might want to be self-conscious for the rest of your life."

BRIAN REGAN

You know what it's like having five kids?

Imagine you're drowning and someone hands you a baby.

JIM GAFFIGAN

Diced Onions

While researching *The Humor Code*, I learned how the satirical newspaper *The Onion* relies on a self-imposed constraint. When working on a new issue, the writers have a meeting where they pitch headlines and get help punching up their ideas. The key constraint is that a writer is not allowed to re-pitch a headline. Ever. Once a headline has been cast aside, it never comes back, no matter how much the writer likes it, or how good or bad the next week's potential headlines may be. The constraint makes *The Onion's* writers work that much harder.

A few headlines that I am happy made the cut:

Drugs Win Drug War

Child Bankrupts Make-A-Wish Foundation with Wish for Unlimited Wishes

Seagull with Diarrhea Barely Makes It to Crowded Beach in Time

Now that you've seen some of the ways comedy benefits from constraints, let's shift our lens to business.

COMMERCE FREED BY CONSTRAINTS

In business, lacking time or money is often a problem. Not having enough time to generate and explore options is truly a problem. Supply chain constraints, distribution constraints, regulatory constraints—they're typically terrible for business.

Nonetheless, constraints spur creative thinking by virtue of extra effort or divergent thinking. Here are some examples of businesses who have done this well.

Skip Ad

People's desire to avoid commercials is nothing new, and yet with more distractions (i.e., that pesky phone) it is harder than ever to capture someone's attention. As a consequence, fifteen-second commercials are more common on television than thirty-second commercials.

Perhaps the most annoying thing about commercials is being required to watch five seconds of a YouTube commercial prior to skipping ahead to your cat video.

The obvious solution is to make those first five seconds so spectacular that a viewer will stick around to watch more. But many advertisers are embracing the constraint and saving money in the process. The solution: jam the most essential information into short, six-second ads (assuming a one-second delay for clicking on "Skip Ad").

The insurance company Geico leaned into the six-seconds-and-skip constraint and made a series of "unskippable" ads that are hard to explain yet hilarious to watch. An actor would say one line that involved the word "savings," then the scene would freeze. The narrator would intone, "You can't skip this Geico ad, because it's already over." Then something in the scene would move slightly—a hand, someone's eyes, a dog—and you begin to realize the film isn't frozen: the people are holding still.[23]

The campaign was not just seriously funny, it was seriously successful. 7.5 million people watched the ads to

---

23   In my favorite, a family of four is frozen around the dinner table when the family's Saint Bernard enters the scene. It sniffs at the food, climbs up on the table, and joyously, noisily, eats everyone's spaghetti, upending plates, stepping in bowls, and wagging its tail in peoples' faces. The actors are doing everything they can to not break character.

the end in the first two weeks. And after it got covered by the media, people sought out the ads...for entertainment.

Not Sweating It

Over the years, Nike has caught hell over its alleged sweatshop-like conditions and has sought to improve conditions. In 2004, one challenge was the glue Nike was using to connect soles to the rest of the shoe. The glue was toxic, but workers were removing their safety masks when they weren't being monitored. The masks were annoying. It was difficult to communicate while wearing them. The factories get hot, so the masks were also uncomfortable.

At first blush, a solution would be to rely on economic theory: use carrots (i.e., rewards) and sticks (i.e., punishments) to force workers to wear the safety masks. But this is costly, impractical, and bad for morale. The solution seems obvious in hindsight. Nike chose to redesign the glue to no longer be toxic.

Sometimes it takes a constraint to make us choose the best option, even if it's not the obvious one.

Little Big Successes

In his book *Small Giants*, Bo Burlingham profiles companies that choose greatness over growth. You probably won't know the names of any of the companies—because they purposefully stay small. This is their self-imposed constraint.

It started twenty years ago with Zingerman's Deli. In an interview with Michelle Darne, he talked about the experience:

> They had been extremely successful and had the opportunity to get very big, to go national, to franchise. They decided they didn't want to do that, because they had other goals they considered more important.

> I was blown away by the creativity of what they did and by the quality of the people that they were able to attract. People from big corporations would take big cuts in salary to go work there. People who'd been partners in national accounting firms would leave in order to go and bake bread at this company.

In the book, Burlingham profiles companies that had the opportunity to grow very big but chose not to because other goals were more important. One of the secrets was that these companies maintained a small enough size that everybody in the company could know everybody else:

By staying small, these companies were able to keep their "mojo"—the charisma that makes them the great companies they are.

IMPLICATION: UNWRITTEN RULES

Rules are protectors of the status quo.

When you think of rules, the rules that come to mind are the ones written down by governments, schools, and HR. Comedians do their fair share of making fun of written-down rules.

Yet, there is another important set of rules to understand.

Unwritten rules aren't written anywhere (hence their name), and yet you know them—and if you aren't aware of an unwritten rule, you'll learn it real quick.

Nearly everything I know about unwritten rules, I have learned from Jeff Leitner. He is *the* expert on unwritten rules and directs Unwritten Labs, which examines how unwritten rules affect organizations. He told me:

> We think we're self-directed and independent, but we're really highly interdependent social creatures. So unwritten rules—the way humans signal and reinforce group behavior—are extraordinarily influential.

Unwritten rules make our groups and our lives stable and predictable. We generally don't have to guess what other people want from us and they don't have to guess what we want from them.

But all that stability and predictability comes at a steep price: unwritten rules make our groups—our families, our companies, our groups of friends—really resistant to change.

These written and unwritten rules become the walls that keep us in the status quo. To step outside brings consequences. Breaking written rules prompts formal punishment, and breaking unwritten rules causes social rejection.

This is where thinking like a comedian can help. A comedian's ability to recognize the status quo—the written and unwritten rules—and call them out allows us to appraise their validity. Which rules are useless, counterproductive, or unjust? Do you agree with the rules you are so dutifully following? Did you even know they existed? What could you accomplish if you stopped playing by the "rules" and started stepping outside of your status quo?

When we look at status quo-smashing businesses like Rent the Runway or Spanx, they make great business sense the moment you hear about them. But many ideas that are a normal part of today's world seemed crazy when first introduced. There was resistance to the automobile, the telephone, and even movies with sound. Harry Warner, one of the founders of Warner Bros famously said, "Who the hell wants to hear actors talk?"

DEVELOP YOUR SHTICK

The world really doesn't want you to step out of the stream. Businesses pay lip service to this idea, but the general sentiment is: don't be *difficult*. This is actually an advantage. That said, as a result, stepping out of the stream can be a delicate situation. You don't need to announce it. Pick your spots, be nice, and see how far you can push your boundary-pushing behavior.

Here are some questions to ask yourself as you contemplate how to apply the ideas in this chapter to your life.

- Can I ask the questions that a humanoid would ask? Keep asking, "Why?"
- Am I in a liminal space? Where are the transitions and breaks from the day-to-day that can expose a new way of thinking?
- What are the written and unwritten rules that I am living with? What are the real versus imagined consequences of breaking this or that rule? Are any of these written and unwritten rules in conflict?

- What decisions really scare you? What bigger risks can you seek out?
- When you encounter a constraint, can you say, "Good. This will give us an opportunity to be more creative"? What constraint can you lean into?

Good businesses and entrepreneurs don't get trapped in the norm or give in to the naysayers. Instead, they spin the status quo upside down to recognize the opportunities that are sitting right there in front of them—in front of us all. Stepping out of the stream, then, begins not in action, but in thought.

Case in point: your next Act Out.

ACT OUT: THIRD THOUGHTS

Creativity is an appropriate, original solution to a problem. "We need to be more creative," really just means, "We need to solve this problem in a way that no one else has yet."

An effective—albeit tedious—way to be creative is through extreme persistence. Most of the time, your first solution is appropriate but not original. And so you must keep trying.

Do you know why Nikki Glaser is so much fun to bring to a roast? She solicits joke ideas from a network of friends—receiving upwards of seventy suggestions to fuel her as she writes the final jokes.

A lack of originality explains what most people in comedy think of as joke stealing. Two comedians tell nearly the same joke. The person who told the jokes first accuses the person who told the joke second.

Just imagine the sprint to the open mic the day Viagra aired its "four-hour erection" warning.

There's a long history of independent invention with technology. For example, on the day Alexander Graham Bell filed for the patent for the telephone, so did Elisha Gray for his version of the telephone. (You can guess who got to the patent office first.)

A key to truly creative and innovative solutions is to ignore your first thought. Have second thoughts. Third thoughts. Even better, have 100 thoughts! Better still, check out the workbook exercise available at PeterMcGraw.org.

SHTICK FROM SHANE

Comedy requires persistence. For every ten jokes I write, one of them makes it on stage. For every ten that makes it on stage, one makes it into my act. For every one that makes it into my act, one makes it on TV or an album. Now, I am not great at math, but Pete should call this the *One Billion Joke Rule*.

CHAPTER 3

CREATE A CHASM

Andy Kaufman grew up in Great Neck, New York to become one of America's most innovative entertainers.

People familiar with Kaufman either love him or hate him. He's either a brilliant, comedic genius, or a baffling, capricious jerk. He was a madman—terribly dedicated to his craft. For his fans, that's precisely why they love him. For his non-fans, that's precisely why they hate him.

When Kaufman first arrived on the comedy scene, it wasn't even clear that he was trying to be funny. In the age when everyone else was telling setup-punchline style jokes, he was doing impressions, singing, dancing, and lip-syncing. Kaufman called himself a song and dance man—a performer.

For example, he would set up a record player next to him on stage and play the *Mighty Mouse* theme song. He'd wait awkwardly until the one line Mighty Mouse himself sings during the refrain: "Here I come to save the day!" And Kaufman would *lip-sync* it. For the rest of the song, he'd wait patiently for his cue, even taking sips of water. I like to use this clip as a demonstration in my professional keynotes. It is enlightening to watch how Kaufman divides the audience. Some smile and laugh. Others are furrowing their brow, confused by the character on the screen. But whether delighted or abhorred, few people are neutral.

One character he did was The Foreign Man, a meek, awkward guy with a squeaky voice and a European-ish accent. The Foreign Man later morphed into his character Latka on the television show *Taxi*.

Another alter-ego of Kaufman's was Tony Clifton, an obnoxious lounge singer that most everyone hated. While Kaufman was on *Taxi*, he negotiated a fascinating contract that stipulated Clifton would have to do a certain number of appearances. One day, as Clifton, he showed up to the set with two prostitutes, demanding they be written into the show. Clifton was escorted off the set and fired. Co-star Tony Danza happened to be recording what was going on behind the scenes of Taxi that day and caught the whole thing on tape.[24]

The next day, the cast gathered in Danza's dressing room to watch the outrageous scene play out. The cast didn't realize that Kaufman had entered the room and was watching as well. After it was over, they saw him and froze, waiting for his response. He shook his head in disappointment and, referring to Clifton, said, "What an asshole." Then he walked out like nothing happened.

It was extremely difficult for anyone, even those he worked closely with, to know when Kaufman was acting. And again, for his true fans, the not knowing was part of the appeal.

MAKE THE SPLIT

Truly memorable comedians don't stop after stepping out of the stream; they push it as far as they can. They step out, draw the proverbial line in the sand, pack it with dynamite, and then blast a crack as wide and deep as the Grand Canyon—haters on one side, true fans on the other.

---

24 Jim Carey played Andy Kaufman in the 1999 film *Man on the Moon*, as well as his alter ego Tony Clifton. Carey's portrayal of each was so real, those who had known Andy (and Tony) in real life said it was just as obnoxious as it'd been the first time. The behind-the-scenes footage of *Man on the Moon*—in which Carey never breaks character—was released as 2017 Netflix documentary *Jim & Andy: The Great Beyond*.

They create a chasm.

Kaufman exemplifies this process and the three major ideas in this chapter: 1) he focused on the people who loved him, and he didn't care about the people who didn't love him; 2) he cut through the clutter with his ability to appear so real and raw; and 3) he wasn't afraid to pick a fight.

To achieve your next-level career goals, perhaps you'll do the same.

DON'T SERVE WARM TEA

As part of a lesson in my MBA class, I present this customer satisfaction figure and ask which brand—A or B—my students would want to manage.

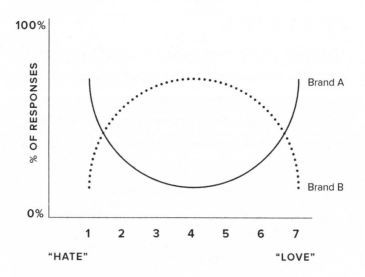

It is a spirited debate. Some of my students prefer to manage Brand A. Most students prefer to manage Brand B.

The "Brand B" crowd: think of being a brand manager for Toyota, Coke, Microsoft, or Capital One. Huge, successful brands that seemingly serve everyone. That's fine, but most successful companies are not like these giants. Moreover, most of these giants didn't behave this way when they first started out.

I contend that my students would benefit from managing Brand A. In that case, you have a sizable proportion of people who love your brand, who will choose your product, and who will engage in positive word of mouth. Further, they are less price sensitive and more loyal—which makes them profitable. Yes, people hate you, but who cares. Your competitors can make them happy.

The data support this assertion. Stocks from companies that create a chasm tend to be more stable in the market than broad companies. Not as high, perhaps, but not as low either. The lovers keep them stable.[25]

In sum: in a world where people want hot tea or iced tea, stop trying to please everyone by serving warm tea.

---

25 Luo, X., Wiles, M., & Raithel, S. (2013). Make the most of a polarizing brand. *Harvard Business Review.*

Comedians are like Brand A.

You know how every other week some comedian is getting in trouble for something they said on Twitter or in a comedy club? As long as the comedian's intended audience is still laughing, those jokes are going to keep coming.

Joan Rivers is Brand A.

Rivers wouldn't serve warm tea. One time, she told a joke about how much she hates children. "The only child that I think I would have ever liked was Helen Keller because she didn't talk." An audience member took offense—not surprisingly. He yelled out that it's not a funny joke if you have a deaf son, which he clearly did. Many people would have backed down or equivocated. Joan did the opposite. The clip is worth watching for her sheer passion, but here's how she responded:

> You are so stupid. Comedy is to make everybody laugh at everything and deal with things, you idiot. My mother is deaf, you stupid son of a bitch. Don't tell me. And just in case you can hear me in the hallway, I lived for nine years with a man with one leg. Okay, you asshole? And we're going to talk about what it's like to have a man with one leg who lost it in World War II and never went back to get it, because that's f*cking littering. So don't you tell me what's funny. Comedy is to make us laugh. If we didn't laugh, where the hell would we all be?

As she later said, "We don't apologize for a joke. We are comics. We are here to make you laugh. If you don't get that, then don't watch us."

This brings us to our first chasm-creating principle.

DIVISIVE TARGETING

If you agree not to serve warm tea, then you will need to figure out who wants hot tea and who wants iced tea. And pick one.

One of the foundational ideas in marketing is to assess the marketplace by looking at needs of customers. These customers are segmented into identifiable groups who have common needs and will respond in the same way to marketing tactics.

You might segment by demographics, psychographics (personality, values), lifestyle (behaviors), or any number of things. Then you choose the group you can *best* serve, and you create products or services to make them happy.

In other words, target them and ignore the others.

READY, AIM, JOKE!

Comedians and successful brands create a chasm

between their target customer and their non-target customer. The work that I have done in the Humor Research Lab confirms this idea. We find that humor arises from benign violations—that is, people laugh at things that are wrong, yet okay. If it is just okay, people are bored. If it is just wrong, people are offended.

The challenge is that what is wrong and what is okay depends on a bunch of individual and cultural variables. The same joke can be funny to one person, boring to a second, and offensive to a third.

Take, for example, the TV show *It's Always Sunny in Philadelphia*. If you are not familiar, it is probably not for you. In an early episode called "Charlie Has Cancer," one of the main characters, well, fakes having cancer. Someone faking having cancer would normally be pure violation. Despicable. But what makes it funny is that Charlie's good friend Dennis is more interested in borrowing a basketball than being sympathetic.

Now, you might not find this funny, but I know the show is funny. Why? Because the show is currently in its fourteenth season. Its fan base *loves* the show.

Good comedy recognizes that if you try to make everyone laugh, then you're more likely to make no one laugh. And when comedians make their target audience laugh

(Benign Violation!), it means their non-target audience will find the things they do completely unfunny—either too benign or too violating. Comedians are very aware of the types of audience their jokes land with, so they maximize laughs by seeking their ideal audience.

SHTICK FROM SHANE

I didn't tell anyone from my hometown that I was moving away to become a comedian. I didn't really think the wholesome folks that I grew up around would get my sense of humor.

The first time anyone from back home saw me do stand-up was when I was going to make my late-night debut on *Conan*.

My grandma played organ in the church a block away from their house and my grandfather sang in the choir. They had been going to this church for probably forty years. So when they found out that their grandson was going to be on TV, my sweet grandma decided to make flyers and hand them out at church so everyone in their little community would watch.

She had no idea that everyone she knew was about to watch her grandson tell sex jokes.

After the debut, my grandparents "coincidentally" started going to a church in a new town.

Do I feel bad for causing my grandparents to leave their church? Yes.

Am I going to write jokes for seniors who would never have any interest in going to a comedy club? Of course not.

WIDE NETS OR AIMED ARROWS

Part of what makes "working clean" so difficult for a comedian is that it must be simultaneously less polarizing and still funny—really funny—enough that it appeals to a wider audience. Stand-up comedian Alonzo Bodden says the hardest job in comedy is to work on a cruise ship. You have to be able to entertain a broad group of people—from widowed grandmothers to young couples. Bodden says that in order to make it on a cruise ship, you better be able to make a doorknob funny.

The business version of cruise ship comedians are essentially the big mass-market brands: Walmart, Coca Cola, or McDonald's. They try to be as broadly appealing as possible. But they are the only ones who can afford to take that approach. When starting out, it's a much better strategy to fearlessly pick your niche and serve it well.

"But Pete, if the biggest and most successful brands are trying to appeal as broadly as possible, isn't that what I should do?"

No. Absolutely not. Being broad is a privilege of the big company with diverse product lines. But those companies didn't start out big—and they didn't start out broad. They begin with a niche. Coca-Cola sold nine drinks a day in its first year. McDonald's started with one store, as did Walmart (i.e., Walton's 5 & 10).

And think about it, these giant brands still create plenty of chasm. Take Starbucks, as an example. Why do people love Starbucks? Because there is a Starbucks on every corner. Because you can get the same Pumpkin Spice Latte wherever you are in the world from Cleveland to Cusco to Cairo.

Why do people hate Starbucks? Because there is a Starbucks on every corner. Because you can get the same Pumpkin Spice Latte wherever you are in the world from Cleveland to Cusco to Cairo.

Not for Everyone

I am doing a sabbatical in California. There is a lot to like about California. There is something for everyone: big cities, beaches, mountains, desert, acupuncture for your dog.

On the other hand, Nebraska doesn't have something for everyone. Sure, you can chase tornadoes or visit the American Museum of Speed in Lincoln, but Nebraska is cited as "so flat you can watch your dog run away for three days."

With that in mind, Nebraska recently changed their state motto...

Nebraska
HONESTLY. IT'S NOT FOR EVERYONE.

And it makes those who it *is* for feel proud.

Too Advanced

If you are a hardcore skier, you probably know Snowbird, the Utah ski resort. With an 11,000-foot summit and more than 3,000-foot vertical drop, it is one of the more exciting mountains in North America. As a company that cares about their customers, the resort monitors reviews. A vocal set of patrons were leaving highly-negative feedback, complaining that "there are no easy runs" and that "the powder is too deep."

These one-star reviews were often from New Yorkers or Angelenos looking for an easier ski experience. Snowbird had a choice at this point. They could take the feedback to heart, groom more of their runs, clear out some trees, and make parts of the mountain easier to ski. (We are pleased to add a new run "Baby's Bottom!")

Alternatively, they could ignore these unsatisfied customers so as not to disappoint their larger number of very satisfied customers who wanted a challenge. Or they could go even further and created a chasm by running an award-winning ad campaign that highlighted the one-star reviews.

You can guess which one they did. For example:

ONE STAR: TOO ADVANCED

I've heard Snowbird is a tough mountain, but this is ridiculous. It felt like every trail was a steep chute or littered with tree wells. How is anyone supposed to ride in that? Not fun!

Greg, Los Angeles, CA

For Snowbird, the difficulty level is their differentiator. They clearly communicated their chasm with a powerful message: Greg, if you want easier runs, go somewhere else.

Pump up the Volume

My favorite example of chasm-creation in business is Barry's Bootcamp.

The high-intensity fitness class features treadmill runs and tough floor exercises. Barry's, which has been around for twenty years, is popular with celebs such as Kim Kardashian and Jake Gyllenhaal. And while Barry's will get you fit, that is not what sets it apart. The workout is similar to its competitors, such as Orange Theory or F45, but the atmosphere is from another world.

First, the space is loud—it's like working out at a nightclub. It is so loud that I asked for earplugs at the front desk. And they had them!

Second, the entire workout space is lit with red lights. This seems strange until you realize how fabulous red lighting makes you look. Amsterdam's Red Light District uses red lights for this same reason.

Third, because the workout and the lights make you look this great, you want to show off. Men will take off their shirts, which is something you don't see at their competitors.

People either love it or hate it. And because of that love, Barry's has been very successful, receiving private equity and expanding outside California and New York into other states and countries.

INCREDIBLY CREDIBLE

Here is one aspect of chasm-creating success you might

not see coming. The most successful businesses and comedians demonstrate hardcore *dedication to authenticity*. People *believe* them and therefore believe *in* them.

Because, no matter how big the chasm, if it's half-hearted it's meaningless. Going all-in is the only way to make it matter. Chasms require commitment.

When you combine authenticity with the principles we've covered so far—creating reversals, taking risks, targeting your ideal audience—you'll produce results with staying power.

AN HONEST DEATH

There's a well-known belief that even the most outrageous comedy contains a sliver of truth. *It's funny cuz it's true.* Therefore a shortcut to creating comedy is to just tell the truth. But—and this will come as no surprise—the truth is often embarrassing.

Doug Stanhope is a crusty, truth-telling, debaucherous comedian. All of the clothes he wears, including those he performs in, he finds in thrift stores. He lives in a compound in a rural Arizona town of 5,192 people.

Stanhope and his mom, Bonnie, shared the same sick sense of humor. When Stanhope was ten years old,

Bonnie took him to Richard Pryor's R-rated stand-up movie. The two had a loving relationship; she always encouraged him to follow his dreams.

By his own admission, Bonnie was an alcoholic, depressive, and a "pill-head," with suicidal tendencies. In 2008, poor Bonnie was dying of emphysema and told him she couldn't go on. He joined her as she took thirty morphine pills, washed down with cocktails. Then he and his friends roasted her while she waited to die. Stanhope even considered hiring a clown, but his small town didn't have one.

He shares the full experience in his memoir *Digging Up Mother—A Love Story*, and his comedy special of the same name. Both the special and book are simultaneously disconcerting, touching, and hilarious (if you like Doug Stanhope).

In the special, he jokes about her generosity from beyond the grave:

> If there were no afterlife, how could my mother have bought me and my friends so many nice things from the SkyMall catalog on her credit card four days after she passed from this Earth?

He waited, of course, to make this joke until after the statute of limitations on credit card fraud ran out.

Stanhope doesn't care about what others think. Does he push things too far? Certainly for some people. But pushing things is authentic to him and part of his comic genius.

SHTICK FROM SHANE

Many times after a successful show, people will come up to me and earnestly ask, "Are you okay?" Audience members are not used to seeing people doing material on suicidal thoughts or spending time in the psych ward.

I learned early on that if I was afraid to talk about something, the audience would reward the courage. The things that I felt vulnerable about were not only different than what audiences would normally hear, but the best comedy can also come from dark yet authentic places.

My rule that I use: when the thought occurs to me that I SHOULDN'T share something on stage, I HAVE TO share it.

BTW, Pete would like me to let you know that I am doing just fine, and the knife he is holding to my throat is there for creative inspiration.

SAY IT LIKE YOU MEAN IT

When it comes to authenticity in business, one way to own your truth and commit to your chasm is through the words you use to communicate with your audience.

Renting Manhattan

When you sell a commodity, the typical way to compete is to lower prices. But then it's just a race to the bottom. If you're selling people space to store their stuff, the battle comes down to who has the cheapest square footage. But when you're selling people extra space in Manhattan, well, there's no such thing as cheap square footage.

Manhattanites looking for more space will move to the suburbs. But Manhattan Mini Storage tries to convince people to stay. Their pitch was that you can keep your tiny apartment and then pay them to store the rest of your stuff that doesn't fit in your space. But in their campaign, they added a healthy dose of famous New Yorker frankness that got them much more respect (and attention):

> The rapture was pushed to October, so no more procrastinating.

> You'll have more wiggle room than [Mayor] Herman's morals.

> Why leave a city that has six professional sports teams, and also the Mets.

They put up billboards and posters around the city like these. The message is impossible to ignore—simultaneously giving people a reason to pick them, and also *not* pick them.

Inspired by Manhattan Mini Storage, I have decided to launch my own billboard campaign. What do you think?

Buy this book. You have nothing to lose but time, money, and your job.

Your teachers are wrong. Listen to the class clowns.

Want to lose weight? This book has no advice for you.

Shock to the System

French Connection, the high-end fashion store for young people, was launched by founder Stephen Marks in 1972, the same year the film for which it is named was released. French Connection UK began using their acronym—FCUK—in their advertising in 1991. The idea arose from faxes being sent between the Hong Kong office and the UK office where the offices names were abbreviated "FCHK" and "FCUK," respectively.

The acronym is pretty impossible to ignore. The company advertised their new London store as "the world's biggest FCUK" and "one humongous FCUK." It wasn't a lie: the location on Oxford Street had more square footage than any other previous store.

They got in trouble from the Advertising Standard Authority (the advertising watchdog) who warned them not to do it again. Yet when the store came to the Golden Gate city they promoted it as "San Francisco's first FCUK."

Marks credited much of the company's success to using the polarizing label. The company leveraged the acronym, putting it on 20 percent of their products.

We Suck

Domino's Pizza is an innovative company. Its "thirty minutes or its free" promise launched in 1979. The company also invented Pizza Tracker in 2008 so that people could see when their pizza was being made, boxed, and sent out for delivery. The tracker pushed people to order online, and when people ordered online, they spent about $2.00 more per order.

But no amount of convenience could bolster the floundering company. Their stock price was at $3 per share, and sales growth was lower than the industry average.

They wanted to get to the bottom of why their brand was trash, so they surveyed their customers. The responses streamed in, and the truth was hard to swallow. Literally.

Domino's food was terrible. The pizza itself—their core product—was rated as the worst among major restaurants.

The sauce was weak and the crust was often described as cardboard. Even Chuck-E-Cheese ranked better on pizza quality.

Rather than whine, Domino's got to work making a better pizza. They rebuilt every recipe, retooled their ingredients and supply chain, and retrained their entire staff. Then they shared their results with the world.

Normally, when a company improves its core product, they run a basic campaign. You've seen them a thousand times. "Now with real bits of bacon!" "Twenty percent more active ingredients!" And of course, "New and improved!"

Not Domino's. In 2010, they ran a campaign that admitted, without mincing their words, "Our pizza sucks. We're sorry. We've made it better. Please tell us if you like it." In fact, they put their president, their head chef, and their marketing director on camera to read the harsh reviews and publicly eat crow.

The campaign included a series of creative marketing communications—ranging from marquees in Times Square to commercials where they visited their most critical customers to have them try the new pizza.

The improvements in the pizza were profound and expensive. They had to change every ingredient and every pizza recipe. But they knew that wouldn't be enough to get people to try them again. Coupling the improved pizza with the mea culpa is what turned everything around. The "Pizza Turnaround" campaign led to positive buzz about the company and increased in-store sales.

By dangerously embracing credibility, Domino's got back in business. At their low point, they had the worst pizza in the industry. They are now the #1 pizza restaurant in the world and their $294 stock price shows it.

Congratulations to the scatterbrained person who forgot to dump their Domino's stock!

PICK A FIGHT

Picking a fight is undoubtedly the most foolproof way to create a chasm. At one point, Andy Kaufman got into wrestling (literally)—claiming he was the intergender wrestling champion of the world. He would wrestle women and offer them money if they won.

Conflict and controversy automatically make people choose a side. They're either with you or they're not. While this may not be the ideal avenue for, ahem, intimate relationships...for comedy and business, it's damn near a sure thing.

FIGHTING THROUGH LAUGHTER

Arguably the best comedian of his generation, Dave Chappelle embodies many of the comedic practices and perspectives covered in this book. Want a better example of stepping out of the stream? He walked away from a $50 million contract offer from Comedy Central.

Like all stand-ups, Chappelle works out new material on the road, subjecting the audience to a mix of half-baked and fully-baked jokes. And like all stand-ups, he would find videos of these bits all over the internet. Fed up with having his jokes broadcast to the world before they were perfected, Chappelle did the thing performers every-where wish they could do: he started requiring comedy clubs to bag their patron's cell phones. After resistance from both clubs ("Crap. We need to buy these bags.") and audiences ("Crap. I can't *live* without my phone."), bagging phones is now a common practice. Everyone benefits: the comedian can take greater risks and the audience is more present and attentive. We owe a debt of gratitude to Chappelle for not caring about our feelings.

That is a small fight, but he doesn't shy away from big fights, either.

Typically, critics are good at judging shows based on their perception of how well the intended audience will like it. Not so in the case of Dave Chappelle's comedy special *Sticks and Stones*. Chappelle's material in the special attacks the rampant rise in "cancel culture." He does an impression:

> Okay, here it goes. Duh, hey, der, if you do anything wrong in your life, duh, and I find out about it I'm going to try and take everything away from you, and I don't care when I find out. It could be today, tomorrow, fifteen, twenty years from now, if I find out, you're f*cking, duh, finished.

> Who is that?

> That's you! That's what the audience sounds like to me. That's why I don't be coming out doing comedy all the time, because...

I can't write what he says next, but I'll say it is not the kind of thing you say to an audience who you want on your side. Yet the audience gives him a long applause break and a cheer.

While the professional critics cited on Rotten Tomatoes give *Sticks & Stones* a 31 percent satisfaction rating, the user audience's score is 99 percent.

Here is an important distinction: critics don't create chasms, they critique them.

Bulletproof Satire

Sacha Baron Cohen is a modern-day Andy Kaufman. The British comedian's outrageous and offensive characters—most notably Borat and Bruno—are so polarizing, and he so fully becomes them, that he often fears people are going to kill him. And not metaphorically.

In 2018, while filming his satirical series *Who is America?* Cohen disguised himself as a liberal speaker and held a public meeting in a small town in Arizona to prank residents by telling them that their town was about to become the building site for the world's largest mosque outside of the Middle East. Cohen had hired a bodyguard for the event in case any of the locals reacted too strongly to the joke. In a town where residents may carry concealed weapons, the bodyguard had to ensure that weapons were removed before people entered the meeting.

"However, some people might [still] have a gun on them," the bodyguard warned Cohen. "Don't worry, if somebody pulls out a gun and tries to shoot you, I've actually created a bulletproof clipboard."

And so, Sacha Baron Cohen carried a bulletproof clipboard the entire day of the shoot. And this isn't even the most bizarre thing that Cohen has done in his career. He ain't scared to pick a fight.

Roast Rage

When I was growing up, busting on each other with your friends was a common pastime and a rite of passage. At some point, someone would move past regular insults and throw down the yo momma jokes—this could make friendly banter nearly come to blows.

Busting was our roasting.

Jeffrey Ross is the king of comedy roasts, and another creator of chasms. He is so committed to his jokes, he's willing to put himself in harm's way. I bet he told some epic Yo Mama jokes as a teenager.

Ross won't just roast someone behind the safety of a podium in a controlled environment. He'll go out into the world, on the street, and stand next to his subjects (i.e., victims), risking not only that he won't get a laugh, but that he'll get punched in the face.

Ross visited the Westboro Baptist Church and was met by two big, burly churchgoers who met him with protest signs. He roasted these two guys to their face. You can watch the video on my YouTube channel.

Spoiler alert: he doesn't get punched, and they were laughing by the end.

BUSINESS BATTLEGROUND

There are so many great stories of brands and people who have said no to warm tea and were unafraid to make an audience choose a side. And they weren't afraid to get hostile or hit that hot-button either. As Seth Godin says, "Go start a ruckus."

Hate Us for a Discount

Davide Cerretini is the owner of Botto Bistro in California. Frustrated at being at the mercy of Yelp, which he felt was extorting small businesses for advertising, he decided to fight back. He put up a sign at his restaurant saying that customers who gave his restaurant a one-star Yelp review would receive 25 percent off their next pizza. Later, he raised the discount to 50 percent.

"Hate us on Yelp" became his ticket to fame. It resulted in 2,300 one-star ratings, and Botto Bistro became the worst-rated restaurant on Yelp. However, most of the one-star reviews complained ironically about how *good* the pizza is:

I wish there was a zero star option. I'd give that to them.

My food arrived before I wanted it to come. It was too hot to eat. It brought back all kinds of terrible memories of eating in Italy.

Cerretini both got his revenge at Yelp and turned into a bit of a celebrity. His restaurant is still in business, and he has gone on to do private cooking lessons for $3,000 a pop.

Inspired by Cerretini, I bought Shane a pizza in exchange for a one-star review of this book:

> Meh. Once you get past this book's terrible title, you realize that's the best part of the book. Seriously, how many fitness examples can a reader stomach? I get it, McGraw, you're jacked.
>
> —SHANE MAUSS, UNSATISFIED CONTRIBUTOR

Believe in Something

Nike gave up on golf equipment years ago, in part because they recognized that in a post-Tiger Woods world, golf is on the decline—especially with young people. Even though golf is still a sizeable business, Nike chases growth.

Dropping golf is one thing, but Nike made a chasm-creating decision to chase growth when they launched their *Believe in Something* campaign with Colin Kaepernick. I have no doubt that you have heard about it. Sure enough, the world split. Some people loved it, and some people set their Nike gear on fire. The campaign was both vilified and celebrated. Their bet on the young and international customer was a smart one: online sales jumped

31 percent, and their stock went up 5 percent (a six-billion-dollar increase in value).

A sporting goods store in Colorado Springs decided to boycott Nike products due to the Kaepernick campaign. A few months later it went out of business. Stephen Martin, owner of the store, later said, "Being a sports store without Nike jerseys is like being a milk store without milk or a gas station without gas."

Semi-Sweet Revenge

From the sixties until the fall of the former Soviet Union, the communist country of Romania had one chocolate bar, called Rom. This was not unusual. In these countries, there was one vodka, one cheese, and one emotion.

But even as the only chocolate bar in town, it was still an acquired taste.

When the doors to the country were open to foreign investment, here came the competition. Rom had a hard time competing with the sweetness of Snickers. Not only was Rom not as tasty, but it was being outspent and out-distributed by its well-funded and feisty competitors.

Romanian-born Adrian Botan was creative director at McCann Erickson Romania at the time. He told me, "One of my dreams was to work for this brand. I wanted to revive it."

In 2010, he led the project to do just that. The goal was to transition the Rom brand into a nostalgia brand, but it was nostalgia with a twist, playing on irony and communism:

> You see, we re-launched Rom as the chocolate that would bring back the memories of the communist era. As those memories were a mixed bag, they would come as "strong and bitter" as in the strong and bitter taste of Rom chocolate.

The campaign made fun of these minor traumas that would have been daily occurrences during communism. A series of commercials depicted Romanians biting into a Rom bar and bringing back some aspect of communist culture. In one, a long-haired man bites into a Rom bar and unwittingly summons the secret communist police squad who stuff him in a car, drive him to a warehouse, and give him a disciplinary haircut. They dump him back on the sidewalk with a freshly shaved head. (It helps to be Romanian to appreciate this bit.)

Each ad ends with the Rom slogan, "Strong sensations since 1964."

The campaign was great for older consumers who would

get a kick out of the tongue-in-cheek callbacks to harder times. But younger consumers didn't care about the old days which they'd only heard from hearsay. Even worse, the younger generation didn't want a lecture on national pride.

Botan and the team realized they needed to "provoke" latent national pride by attacking its symbol. They would take away the existing Romanian flag coloring on the package and replace it with an enemy. The Russian flag was considered but deemed too offensive (pure violation), and so instead they went with the American flag, because the USA had both positive and negative associations.

Changing the packaging was a bold move for the Rom company. Botan and his peers had to convince management to take the risk. They used the example of the non-staged crisis of New Coke, where customers demanded their "old" Coke back.

Of course, with Rom it was going to be different. The goal was to intentionally create a crisis, and then solve it. Rom set up a war room to prepare for the impending crisis. It's a strange day when you are intentionally trying to upset your customers. The plan was secret—the majority of employees didn't know about it. When the factory workers found out about the change, they were outraged. Botan recalled, "They wanted to kill the management."

Rom got precisely what they were hoping for: a national outcry, now referred to as *Romanian reactive patriotism*. A week of Facebook comments, YouTube videos, a flash mob, and talk show coverage.

The final stage was to bring back the original branding with Romania's colors. Picking the fight paid off. Rom sales saw an 80 percent rise in market share to the #1 position in the category, and the Rom chocolate bar became iconic.

IMPLICATION: FLAW OF AVERAGES

Good businesses constantly monitor their customer satisfaction scores—on the lookout for problems. You see, customer satisfaction is an indicator of customer loyalty, but the former is easier to measure.

Most customer satisfaction scores are presented as a summary number. Take for example the Net Promoter Score (NPS). The Net Promoter Score asks customers to rate on a scale of 0 to 10 how likely they are to recommend a specific business to someone else. Ranges of scores represent detractors (0-6: those who think negatively of you), passives (7-8: they could take or leave it), and promoters (9-10: fanatics who shout your praises from the rooftops). Or so they claim.

☹ ☹ ☹ ☹ ☹ ☹ ☹ | 😐 😐 | ☺ ☺

| 0 | 1 | 2 | 3 | 4 | 5 | 6 | 7 | 8 | 9 | 10 |

Detractors | Passives | Promoters

☺% − ☹% = NET PROMOTER SCORE

The NPS subtracts detractors from promoters to give you a "net" score. But the thing is, you can't be looking at how much people like you "on average," because average is not the truth. The problem with the NPS is it throws away valuable data by giving you a single score. Instead, you need to see the distribution of responses. A one-hump distribution is radically different from a two-hump distribution.

Rather than looking at averages, you want to look at frequencies—the numbers that make up the average. What is happening with the people who *love* you?

Remember, the power of the chasm is in not compromising. It's in making people simultaneously love and hate you. Don't waste time and energy trying to raise the low numbers. Instead figure out what you're already doing to attract those weirdos who love you, and then do more of it.

DEVELOP YOUR SHTICK

Because of advances in technology, expansion of the economy, and healthy competition in most categories, nowadays it's pretty easy to get high-quality products and services. Especially with mature product lines, all competitors have already made the major improvements in the category. Once brands leveled up from the flat-footed insoles of Chuck Taylors to a legitimate arch-supporting athletic shoe, there wasn't a whole lot more they could do to make it better. Today, all credit cards offer pretty much the same key features: cashback rewards, great introductory rates, fraud protection, and the like.

Especially if the products or services are largely undifferentiated in your category, look for bolder chasm-creating ways to attract customers.

To help create a chasm, here are some questions to ask yourself:

- Who is your ideal customer? Really, who is that person? What is their profile?
- Can you lean into a controversy? Are you willing to stand your ground for the customers who most love your products?
- Can you double down on things that your true fans love?

- What hard choices can you make to *not* be something for everyone?
- How can you make customers choose? Are you with us or against us?
- And of course: are we serving warm tea?

Next up, the Act Out will take you through a distinct way to create a chasm that may strangely have wide appeal. And then, in chapter four, it will be time to stop picking fights and start making friends.

ACT OUT: AN AUDIENCE OF ONE

When you're trying to create a chasm, one of the challenges is overcoming the fear of disappointing people or making them angry. But angering and disappointing people is, in fact, a reasonable risk. You want something that your target audience can love, even if that means other people hate it.

The radical extension of the notion of creating something that people love is to create something that *only one person* loves. And that one person is you.

Comedians almost always begin their joke-writing process by focusing on things *they* find funny. Only after that, do they worry about building a bridge to the audience—if at all.

Something like this can also happen in business: making something that you personally need to solve a problem.

This is a high risk, high reward scenario. The risk is that it may only solve the problem of one person (i.e., you). But the reward is a special form of creativity that is unlike anything anyone else is doing. And it's a big world— nearly eight billion people big. If you make something that makes *you* happy, there's a good chance that there is a market out there for a portion of that big world who will love it, too.

SHTICK FROM SHANE

Even though comedy is subjective, there is still plenty of room for shared tastes. I used to have a joke about having a sex change and then traveling back in time to get impregnated by myself. When I told it, I would get more weird looks than laughs. But I was convinced it was funny. Comics seemed to like it, but no audience ever laughed at it, so I rarely used it except to amuse myself.

During the recordings of my first comedy album, I had a perfect recording after the first try, so I decided to take some chances on the second recording. I did a bunch of my weirdest material including this joke. It was one of the few times it ever got a laugh.

I liked it enough to put it in the album. When people reviewed the album, they often noted it as the best bit. Then I realized something about what audiences pretend to like and what they actually like. In a live show, club audience members are tuned into what everyone else in the room is laughing at. They don't want to be the person who doesn't get a joke or the only one laughing at the weird joke about a sex-changing time traveler impregnating themselves. However, when listening by themselves in their car, a person is more free to laugh—especially because the funniest jokes are often the least comfortable to laugh at publicly.

Stuart Butterfield is not great at making video games, but he is a master of transforming an aspect of his video game into a profitable business. A really profitable business, one of them worth, say, $7 billion dollars.

In 2002, Butterfield and friends started a company to build a web-based multi-player video game called *Game*

Neverending. The game did end, but one of the features—that allowed you to share photos with other players—had staying power. The tech was amazing, and in 2003, Flickr gave the world a glimpse of what Web 2.0 would become. Flickr was eventually sold to Yahoo! for more than $20 million dollars.

After doing his time at Yahoo!, Butterfield and his team tried again to create a web-based multi-player game called *Glitch*. Unfortunately, the game was too strange, and it couldn't keep players playing—which is kind of important when a game is based on having lots of people playing at once. Because Butterfield and his three co-founders lived in different places (two in Vancouver, one in New York, and one in San Francisco), they were using Internet Relay Chat (IRC) to communicate. However, because IRC was an old technology (built in 1989), the team started to fix up the program to meet the needs of the growing, distributed team. By the end, they had a group chat function on steroids, which allowed for easy, fast, and searchable conversations within an organization. It even replaced email.

They called it Slack. It's an incredible product—one with a 93 percent retention rate.

Creating for an audience of one is a high-risk strategy—it could result in a whole lot of nothing. You see a lot of these ideas on *Shark Tank* that never really get traction. Or it could turn out like Flickr or Slack.

CHAPTER 4

COOPERATE TO INNOVATE

Merrill Markoe is not likely a name you know, but for the past forty years she has made things that are well known.

Markoe is an accomplished comedy writer and creative soul. She's written ten books, and when I met with her in her Malibu home, she was working day and night on the artwork for a graphic novel.

But for most of her career, she was the genius behind the scenes.

Markoe came to Los Angeles in the late '70s and became a researcher and writer for the show *Laugh-In*. At one point, she went down to the Comedy Store on the Sunset

Strip to work out some jokes on stage. The "Store," as it is known in the comedy world, was building its reputation as a premier comedy venue. It was frequented by young talents like Robin Williams, Richard Pryor, Jay Leno, and Andy Kauffman. Her opener was, "the absurdist surrealist kind of joke that you either got or you didn't":

> I was kind of a lonely kid. I didn't have a date for the senior prom so my father made my brother take me. But it worked out okay. My brother and I are getting married. We got a house in the valley. We are going to settle down and raise mutants. Well, there's nothing else to do in the valley anyway.

It got a nice laugh. Markoe, though, didn't quite have the stage presence required to make it as a big-time stand-up.

The Comedy Store is also where she met David Letterman. Letterman had no problem with stage presence. Having grown up in Indiana, he brought an undercurrent of Midwestern folksiness that put people at ease just before he hit them with his sharp wit and biting sarcasm. Before moving to Los Angeles, he'd been a radio talk show DJ, and he could fill hours with impromptu conversation. He was a talented improviser, but he was only an adequate stand-up. That changed when Markoe started writing jokes for Letterman.

Together they went on to accomplish amazing things.

They started out on a TV morning show—sixty minutes, five days a week—with Letterman hosting and Markoe producing. It was her job to make sure they had content to fill the time. And it was here that she created many of the segments they would later feature on *The Late Show*.

She invented "Stupid Pet Tricks" (e.g., pit bulls bowling, cattle dogs jumping double dutch). This led to "Stupid Human Tricks" (e.g., a woman who can make her eyes bug out). They were going to add "Stupid Baby Tricks," but they realized parents couldn't be trusted.

Markoe was fantastic at crafting segments that played to Letterman's strengths. He was admittedly not a very good actor, so they chose not to do the typical sketch comedy skits that most other shows were doing. Instead, she pulled on Letterman's conversational skills honed from his years in radio and sent him out to mingle with strangers. These became his signature "Man on the Street" interviews—improvised and unedited, with glorious mistakes left in.

Markoe and Letterman dated for many years. But it was their comedy partnership that was most fruitful. While Markoe was head writer, *Late Night with David Letterman* won five Emmys for outstanding writing. Pretty good on their own, they became fantastic when they teamed up.

Great comedy isn't a solo venture—it's a collaboration.

THE KNOWN GENIUS

The legend of the lone genius is overblown.

Whenever you look into the shadows behind success, you will almost always find someone behind the scenes who helps turn the almost famous into the famous. This special someone (or several someones) contribute essential skills behind the scenes.

Without Neal Brennan, there's no *Chappelle's Show*. Without Larry David, there's no *Seinfeld*.

For David Letterman, the guy behind the guy was a gal name Merrill Markoe—without her there's no Emmys for *Late Night with David Letterman*.

The collaboration works because the collaborators are alike enough to understand each other but different enough to combine their skills in complementary—and funny—ways. This is also true of science, technology, and of course, business.

And yet far too many people falsely expect to be able to do it on their own—and then become discouraged when they can't. The myth of the lone genius ruthlessly takes root and creates a false narrative that is actually counterproductive to creativity and innovation.

One point for clarity: the terms creativity and innovation are often used interchangeably, but they are not synonymous. Creativity occurs when you arrive at an *original, appropriate solution* to a problem. Innovation occurs when you *execute that solution*. While you may find a lone genius (or mostly-lone genius) on the creative side (i.e. generating an original idea), you almost never find one alone on the innovation side (i.e. bringing the idea to life). Innovation requires cooperation.

To create groundbreaking innovations, we must reject the myth of the lone genius, and harness the power of group genius.

INVENTIONS OF MYTH

Thomas Edison's legend was built on the back of a large team that tirelessly worked through thousands of possible inventions. Edison needed a large team because he knew that most early prototypes for any invention would fail. Edison welcomed failure so that he could learn what would *not* work. So he employed a group big enough to explore as many possible solutions as possible (Ahem. Third thoughts.). We don't remember Edison's failures. And we certainly don't remember his team.

Steve Jobs's incredible return to Apple was built largely on three banging inventions: iPod, iPad, iPhone. A mastermind of design, everything he touched seemed to turn to gold. But Jobs relied on teams at Apple to execute his vision.

Despite his world-changing success, I believe that Steve Jobs was lucky to reach his level of success, because he missed opportunities to foster teamwork. I realize this is heretical to people who adore Jobs, but here's an example.

Imagine the complexities of inventing the iPhone. From the hardware to the software, it was a daunting engineering task. A six-person team labored in a challenging, high-pressure environment. One team member gained fifty pounds during the iPhone's development from stress and lack of exercise. Another member of the team had the bad luck of sharing the first name as Jobs: Steve Lemay. This caused a problem when Lemay answered questions directed to Jobs. One day in a fit of frustration, Jobs told Lemay that his name could no longer be Steve.

Now, it's very easy to imagine a variety of alternative names he could go by: Steven, Stevesie, Steve-O, Lemay, or Champ. All would be acceptable. But no, Jobs doesn't do this.

Jobs declares, "You're no longer Steve. You're now Margaret."

This is what he told a key member of the team—a high-level, critical player. Jobs was lucky Lemay *is* a champ. Even though he was so talented he could work anywhere he wanted, he didn't tell Jobs to take his job and shove it.

Despite outbursts and antics like this, Apple was able to invent the iPhone. Imagine what Jobs could have done if he had a bit better rapport with his collaborators. Don't @ me.

GENERATING GROUP GENIUS

At the beginning of the book, I introduced the three pillars of comedy: stand-up, sketch, and improv. Each has its own form of cooperative interaction.

IMPROV

If you've ever seen an improv show at Groundlings, Second City, or Upright Citizens Brigade, there is often an improviser on stage that is head and shoulders above the rest. Someone who seems like a comedic genius. You leave the show thinking, "Wow, that person is so good. Why aren't they ditching these clowns for the big leagues?"

But if you attend that show repeatedly, the so-called genius usually changes from week to week. This makes sense if you understand the way that improv teams work to create a scene—and subsequently comedy—out of nothing.

The structure of improv allows for extreme levels of cooperation among the members. It is such a difficult process that there are explicit, agreed-upon rules designed to enhance cooperation. Things like: "Yes, and..." "Make statements." "Don't pimp out your partner." Many of these rules lead actors to subordinate themselves in service to the scene. They do what's required to build a scene, create comedic tension, and to help the scene move forward. In any given week, when someone shines as a genius, they shine in large part because their scene partners are setting them up to shine. As an improv actor, you don't know who is going to stand out in any one scene or any given night—including yourself.

As a business person you may have heard of "Yes, and." This improv rule has been making the rounds through the business circuit for several years now. Building an entertaining scene out of nothing—the basis for improv—is really difficult. It requires that the performers agree with (i.e., "yes") and build upon (i.e., "and") each other's ideas.

Beyond its utility for improv and for business, this is a useful rule for life. Because the rule is already so well-known, we will look past "Yes, and" to develop cooperative genius.

SKETCH

Sketch is a fundamental form of comedy writing: creating two- to six-minute scenes built on an amusing premise. A sketch group might have an equal number of writers and actors (e.g., six of each), and each writer will be responsible for leading a different sketch.

If you're the lead writer, you might develop the premise for the sketch (the creative idea), but your fellow writers will help you fix the story structure, punch up jokes, and sharpen the characters. Then you hand the script over to a director and actors who will bring it to life. So even if it's your premise and your writing, the execution of your sketch relies on the eleven other people on the team.

Barnet Kellman is an Emmy-award-winning comedy director of TV sitcoms such as *Murphy Brown.* Nowadays, Kellman co-directs the comedy program at USC's School of Cinematic Arts. (I am a visiting scholar there as I finish this book.) Kellman views the director as the midwife of the actor's performance, a concept he teaches his students. As he sees it, together they are "having" a baby. "The director is there to create a comfortable, safe environment; coach; reassure; and intervene only when needed." This is because even a genius actor needs a comforting hand sometimes. And a genius director has to let someone else do their work. Everyone has a job:

The actors are doing the actions and saying words. The writer wrote the script. The lighting people are lighting, somebody else is shooting. My job is to create the conditions where they can all do their best, while gently guiding them in the same direction.

STAND-UP

A lone wolf travels the country, standing alone under a spotlight, and telling jokes that he or she wrote. The stand-up comedian may seem like the exception to the premise that innovation requires collaboration.

Yet even stand-up comedians need others to innovate. First, stand-ups are often reliant on fellow comedians for feedback and motivation. When comedians don't know each other, they will congratulate each other after a show by saying, "Nice set." But when they are friends, they will do an in-depth post-mortem after a show, working through bits and helping with punch-ups.

And every stand-up comedian, even the most lone-wolf-like, needs an audience. There is only one real way to know that they've actually hit their mark: is the audience laughing? The audience is not just their customer; they're a key collaborator.

The stand-up comedian is constantly testing and refining their work in open mics and drop-in comedy club sets—low stakes environments. But their big unveiling is typically a comedy special.

To prepare for an hour-long comedy special, the comedian will have spent upwards of a year writing, testing out, and honing this material in front of hundreds of audiences. Comedy specials, therefore, are usually very polished and get big, consistent laughs from the audience. You can thank those thousands of previous audience members because there's a good chance they enjoyed the set less than the present crowd.

An audience is so important that comedian Maria Bamford looks for additional opportunities to test out her jokes prior to her show. After landing in a city for a set of weekend shows, she will tweet a message to local fans asking if someone wants a "one-on-one" show hosted at a café, where she pays for "chow and drinks." She uses that time to work on her material and get an up-close reaction to her bits.

A lone wolf doesn't pay for a stranger's drinks.

SHTICK FROM SHANE

We can't be afraid to tell people when things are bad.

In comedy, acquaintances blow smoke up your ass, but friends roast each other. The heat forges the sword. (You will soon find out how much Pete likes sword metaphors.)

Your true friends don't support your worst work, because it hurts you and the audience. It's better to give honest feedback so they can truly punch up the joke or can it from their act.

Would you let someone go on a date or a job interview with spinach in their teeth and toilet paper stuck to their shoe? It might be uncomfortable to tell someone they have a booger in their nose, but the world is better off when you do.

An added benefit of overcoming your reluctance to critique a joke is that it requires the joke teller to think more deeply about how much they care and how they might improve the joke.

You have no idea how much I fought Pete to keep that booger references in this book.

TEAMWORK DREAMWORK

Del Close, one of the fathers of improv, had a saying, "You are all supporting actors." Improv sizzles if each actor supports the other actors, going where they lead, building on their ideas, and giving them what they need in a scene. So even the superstars of improv, such as Amy Poehler or Jimmy Fallon, look good because the people around them are setting them up to shine as a star on stage.

"We are all supporting actors" is consistent with a saying that is so common it has become a proverb: "If you want to go fast, go alone. If you want to go far, go together." And you can bet this applies to so much more than improv.

ON THE SEVENTH DAY, THEY RESTED

Trey Parker and Matt Stone have gone about as far as you can in comedy. They created a long-running, Emmy-winning, animated television show that you may have heard of: *South Park*. Their Broadway play *The Book of Mormon* won nine Tony Awards. Hell, they even made an incredibly funny movie, *Team America*, starring puppets.

I'll say it again. PUPPETS. What *can't* these guys do?

Even more impressive is that an episode of *South Park* is made in six *days*. For comparison, an episode of *The Simpsons* is made in nine *months*.

For my podcast, I sat down with South Park's animation director Jack Shih. He clarified my understanding of how fast the show is made. "Actually, it's five (days) because nothing really gets done on day one."

The South Park team pushes the limits. Shih pondered, "Maybe we can do it in four and a half." The "we" in this scenario is seventy-five people. That includes the accountants. Nothing happens without money.

It's such a tight schedule that when someone gets up from their desk, Shih will ask, "Where are you going? Can you finish the task before you pee?" Shih's not a hardass. He just knows that five minutes is crucial because many other people on the team are waiting for the person to finish so they can move the episode further along.[26]

It's an intense atmosphere. It's not always a happy place, but this is a place where people get along—and they need to get along.

Creative groups are like good family—they don't always agree, but there is a fondness there and understanding of the greater good. It's okay to be a little bit ornery, a little bit of a contrarian, and you need to hold people's feet to the fire in order to get things done. But you also need to be gracious, thank people, and be kind a lot of the time.

In the world of comedy, especially in improv, there is no, "I'm more important than you." We're all supporting actors—and Trey Parker, Matt Stone, *and* Jack Shih have to be decent and kind enough to the people they support.

---

26 *South Park's* team has only missed one deadline in 26 years, and that was due to a four-hour power outage.

This leads us nicely into our next essential element of innovation.

DON'T BE AN ASSHOLE

While it's fun to find TV shows where the actors or writers hate each other, the successful groups almost always get along. They are happy, have fun, and have genuine affection for each other. It's tough to make laughs with someone you hate. So when hater groups do exist, it's more often in dramas than comedies.

Mike Reiss is a long-time writer and one-time showrunner of *The Simpsons*. He told me that in all his years writing for the show, they've had one and a half bad days. Otherwise, people get along. He shared a story with me about a difficult writer that was pulled aside by the showrunner and told that he needed to get along with others or he would be fired.

The writer's response: "Let me think about it." Then he went home for the night.

He came back the next day with his answer. "I discussed it with my wife, and she agreed I can't stop being an asshole."

We should all be so lucky in love.

Bob Sutton, a Stanford professor of organizational behavior, studies assholes. He has documented his research in his books *The No Asshole Rule* and *The Asshole Survival Guide.*

He tells me, "The sheer weight of empirical evidence is overwhelming of the cost of all things asshole—bullying, disrespect, incivility. It causes other people to shut down."

Over and over, Sutton finds that successful work environments benefit from both hiring good people and getting rid of bad people. The benefit of getting rid of one destructive star employee far outweighs the cost. Michael Houseman and Dylan Minor studied the cost of toxic colleagues.[27] They use a dataset of more than 50,000 workers to reveal that moving away from a toxic worker (or simply making a toxic worker "average") enhances productivity to a greater degree than replacing an average worker with a superstar worker (i.e., someone in the top 1 percent of productivity).

---

27 Houseman, M. & Minor, D. (2015). Toxic Workers. Harvard Business School. Working Paper 16-057.

SHTICK FROM SHANE

Let me tell you about something that happens in comedy clubs around the country. The club manager will ask the staff, "Who should we have back?" And guess who the wait-staff asks for?

Of course the staff want comics who fill the room and bring an audience that tips well. But the staff will also ask for the comics who are fun to hang with after the show, who treat them nicely, and are fun to be around.

Truth be told, when I stopped drinking and hanging out after shows, I lost a lot of work!

A COMEDIAN HAS TWO FACES

In the 1950s, sociologist Erving Goffman explained a common dichotomy in the way people manage their daily lives, using the theater terms "front stage" and "backstage." Few people behave the same in public as they do in private. In a way, people behave like actors. They engage in "front stage" behavior when they are out in public and know that people are watching. Then once they're in a private setting—backstage—they reveal their true selves.

He didn't define backstage as being alone or being at home. Rather the backstage of your life is simply the place or places where you feel you can let your guard down, take off your public mask, and be yourself. This could be at home, at the salon or bar with best friends, or at work with your closest colleagues.

Successful comedians may be uncivilized on stage, but they don't get very far if they behave that way backstage. While researching *The Humor Code*, we met Chris Mazzilli, co-owner of Gotham Comedy Club. He doesn't mind if you're a jerk on stage (as long as you're getting laughs), but he doesn't want you to be a jerk to his club manager, bartenders, or any of his staff. In his view, there are plenty of talented people. Why work with a talented jerk when you can work with equally-talented non-jerks?

This principle is made abundantly clear when we look at the careers of several hall of fame comedians—Bill Murray, Steve Martin, even David Letterman. Now in their sixties and seventies, they are still thriving in the entertainment industry.

But not Chevy Chase.

You many know Chase from his National Lampoon *Vacation* films and physical slapstick during his time at *SNL*, and most recently as a non-traditional student at the community college on the show *Community*.

Chase's front-stage persona is a lot like the doofy but earnest character Clark Griswald from *Vacation*. His back-stage persona, evidently, isn't as affable. From poorly-executed racial jokes, to contentious critiques, even fistfights—the word is out, and people are not interested in hiring him anymore.

Whether front stage or backstage, it's crucial to be supportive. And if you can create a culture where everyone is doing that, you have a chance to build something special.

FRIENDS IN HIGH (AND LOW) PLACES

Stand-up comedians need stage time. This means they need other comedians. To get opportunities to practice and test new material, comedians start by hosting their own shows and open mics. They'll put a lineup together, bring in other comedians who can deliver, and get some stage time themselves. Now hosts can invite other comedians who need stage time, often in a quid pro quo manner. When the other comedians host their own shows, they'll return the favor.

Then as comedians start proving they have chops and making more comedy connections, they can get recommended to bookers, clubs, and festivals. Word of mouth and a personal referral goes a long way in the world of comedy. When a booker has a trusted comedian vouching for someone—that they can deliver laughs front stage and get along backstage—that means a lot more than looking at a sizzle reel that cherry-picks a few stellar bits.

Having a friend in the biz goes a long way.

SHTICK FROM SHANE

A lot of times in comedy, a comedian gets buzz within the industry before they get buzz outside of it. When I started out, I received a lot of encouragement from fellow comics and made a lot of new friends. We would have writing meetings together, and I was even in a sketch group for a bit. Comics got me my first spots at real comedy clubs. Comics helped get me into my first comedy festival (The Boston Comedy Festival). That is where a comic saw me and later got me into the biggest festival in the country (Aspen Comedy Festival) At that festival, I won an award, got representation, and booked my first TV spot.

You never know how relationships might benefit you. I have pretended to be friends with Pete for years. It has NOT been easy. But now I am in a book being read by *dozens* of people.

At this point, I hope it's clear that it's difficult to succeed alone. You need other people. And this might mean you need to meet new ones. Ikea instructions tell you to find a friend for some assembly jobs. Unfortunately, Ikea doesn't include instructions for making friends. Luckily, there's a way to meet new people in business.

Yes, I'm talking about networking.

If the concept of networking scares you, start thinking about it differently. Sarah Zaslow, UX Researcher at Google, taught me to look at networking in a new way. Early in her career, she worked with a colleague who was the consummate networker:

("No," he told me.)

> I saw for the first time that good networking was more about communicating genuine interest and care, understanding what other people need, and giving it to them before (or instead of!) asking for what you need. And that it involved having multiple interactions over a period of time, and building a relationship. In other words, it was much more like a friendship than a manipulation or a "trading favors" transaction. On a personal level, I was more comfortable with that frame. After all, I know how to be a good friend. I've been practicing since elementary school!

People dislike networking, but people like making friends. And making friends is what networking truly is: finding a point of connection and pointing it out. Then build from there. What is more fun than nerding out over shared interests? So instead of letting networking turn your stomach, treat it like talking about your favorite movie with people who feel the same way. Or as Zaslow taught me...

Make business friends.

But not only do you need other people, you need to be able to work together. When it comes to cooperation, there is one essential skill that is so obvious it is often overlooked. In fact, I missed it until a veteran cooperator pointed it out.

HEAR HERE

As a novice improviser, I have a lot to learn. The philosophy that we are all supporting actors is a helpful concept, both on and off stage. It simultaneously eases the pressure (I don't have to figure this whole thing out myself) and increases the pressure (I've got to show up with my best for others every time).

Another concept I learned in Improv 101 is called *gifting*. One scene partner sets up another with a useful nugget of information for the person to use to build a scene.

For instance, imagine your partner says, "I'm going to meet BJ for lunch." If you say something like, "Oh, where are you going?" you've added nothing to the scene. You're simply asking for them to do more work: come up with some interesting location to eat.

But imagine if instead you say, "BJ is such a nice person. I'll never understand why you two broke up." You've added new information to the scene—about your partner, about BJ, even about you (you don't get the reason for the breakup). This is more fertile territory to develop the scene's "Who. What. Where."

I had Will Hines on my podcast to talk about improv. Hines is a 20+ year improviser and teacher for Upright Citizens Brigade. I shared my fondness for the concept that "we are all supporting actors" and my positive opinion on gifting. I was surprised when Hines cut me off and said, "Nah, gifting's not really that important."

To Hines, gifting is like a bounce pass in basketball: useful but not essential. As a novice improviser, I appreciate a gift. But the better you get at improv, the less you rely on gifts from others. As an advanced improviser, Hines doesn't need gifts to be successful. If need be, he can take the ball straight to the hoop. Hines is so good, in fact, that his teammates will test him by slinging him anti-gifts (extra-challenging situations) because they want to see him work his magic.

Then what is an essential skill for more experienced improvisers? According to Hines—and this is tough to argue with—it's listening.

Listening is like athletic ability in basketball. You aren't going to get very far without it.

A good improviser is listening to what your other players are saying—which is hard when you're thinking about what you are about to say.

A good improviser is listening for what other players need in order to support them. Do they need someone to move the action along? Are they spent and need an easy way to exit the scene?

A good improviser is also listening for what the scene needs. Does it need more tension? Some slapstick? Something human and emotional to make the action more relatable?

When you're in the midst of creating a scene, it's difficult to be thinking about what you're supposed to do and also pay attention to everyone else. Remember, the crazy thing about improv is that it's made up on the spot. Improvisers write the line a split second before its delivery.

But listening is where the deeper work happens—the work that makes real progress.

LISTENING FOR NOW AND LISTENING FOR LATER

Listening is more than just using your ears. It's about paying attention. There are two types of active listening.

Listening *for now* means listening in the moment. This helps with improvising, adjusting on the fly, and adapting. Listening *for later* is listening for the future. This helps with planning, strategy, and pivoting.

Listening for Now

Performing comedy in front of an audience gives you in-the-moment feedback. The audience is like your teammate, and you both work together to create the best show possible. Some comedians use this to help them with future shows, and others use it to help them craft the show in the moment.

Comedy legend George Burns smoked a cigar onstage. The cigar was a tool. After he delivered a punch line, he could enjoy the cigar while the audience laughed. It allowed him time to listen and think of what he wanted to say next. There's no such thing as an awkward pause when you're suavely puffing a stogie.

Aussie comedian Wil Anderson (who you'll get to know in chapter six) no longer uses a set list for his stand-up shows.[28] Anderson feels like having a set list locks down his material, and he wants the freedom to adjust his set on the fly according to the audience.

---

28   A set list in comedy is the same as at a concert; it lists the jokes that a comedian will tell and in what order.

I don't want to launch into a bit about how I don't like going to the gym and then suddenly, I discover I'm in a room full of people who love going to the gym—and I've still got four and a half minutes of jokes left about this gym. Now I am pushing uphill much more than I've ever pushed (a weight) at the gym.

Comedian Todd Barry remixed stand-up as improv for his Crowd Work Tour. If you've ever seen stand-up, you've seen crowd work. It usually starts when the comedian asks a question to someone in the front row. "Where are you from?" "Are you two together?" "Why are you wearing a winter jacket indoors?" Barry created his entire set by talking to the audience and making up jokes in the moment. Crowd work requires listening to what the audience member is saying, listening to how the rest of the audience is reacting to that interaction, and listening for the chance to create callbacks to earlier jokes made by other comedians.

SHTICK FROM SHANE

Most comics started by performing their memorized material in a heavily scripted way. Comedy is hard, and in the beginning most comics want to do everything perfectly. This, however, can come off as robotic and contrived. Once a comic gets comfortable enough at that, it opens up the possibility of going off-script. It took me years to start to deviate from my planned jokes, but making the switch helped me become a more dynamic and flexible performer. Now rather them talking AT audiences, I'm talking TO them. Bringing them in like a friend sharing stories around a campfire. It's a lot more genuine and connects on a more personal level.

If you don't believe me, read the above paragraph in C3PO's voice.

Listening for Later

Not everything can or should be an in-the-moment observation. Many things take planning and strategy to be their best.

Comedian Janae Burris makes a point to "listen" to her crowd before the start of each show. She will look out in the audience to see who is there, and what they are wearing. She will see if they are drinking beers or martinis. She is paying attention to clues for which material to choose to better suit that audience's tastes and mood.

The Marx Brothers also knew a fair bit about adjusting

material. One of the greatest examples of a hall of fame comedy career, their work spanned Vaudeville to theater to film. Five of their thirteen movies are in the top 100 comedy films by the American Film Institute.

While their movies are the Marx Brothers' greatest success, not everything went smoothly. The Marx Brothers released their first five films with Paramount Pictures. The fifth film was *Duck Soup,* which many critics consider to be the best comedy film of all time. I spoke to Steve Stoliar, who was Groucho Marx's assistant late in Groucho's life and author of the book *Raising Eyebrows.* He told me about how the brothers would make their films:

> The brothers were used to delivering jokes to live theater audiences and would naturally pause for the laughs to subside when on stage. But without cues from the audience, they would have too many jokes too fast in their movies. Bang. Bang. Bang. The movie audience would miss jokes because they were laughing over subsequent punch lines.

Duck Soup underperformed at the box office, and Paramount didn't pick up their option. The brothers toyed with the idea of returning to Broadway, where audiences appreciated them and wouldn't critique them in the way that studios would. This is where it gets interesting:

Irving Thalberg, who was running MGM (the movie studio) in the '30s, was playing bridge with Chico (one of the Marx Brothers), and he told Chico, "I could make a movie with you and your brothers that would have half as many laughs and make twice as much money."

The Marx Brothers signed on. Prior to filming, Thalberg had the Marx Brothers go on the road to perform some of the scenes live. Thalberg wanted to ensure that the laughs were timed well with the scenes and that none of the jokes were drowned out by laughter from the prior joke. Stoliar told me more about the process.

> They had the writers sitting in the audience taking notes. This got a big laugh; this didn't go over well. They would revise the dialogue and they were able to leave room for the laughs such that if you watch *Night At The Opera* by yourself, it seems slow because there are moments when Chico and Groucho are looking at each other after saying something, and it isn't because they forgot the next line. It's because they're leaving room for the laugh there for their audience.

The Marx Brothers' MGM films were their best in terms of production value and pacing. By listening more they made their biggest moneymaker.

PUTTING EARS TO WORK

Listening is a special case of paying attention. Obviously, this practice also applies to commerce.

Business guru Simon Sinek tells a story about Nelson Mandela's renowned leadership skills. The average leader-manager-CEO-parent-coach presents a solution to a problem and asks what the group thinks about that solution. Not Mandela. He would state the problem and ask the group what they thought he should do. It was only after everyone had a chance to speak, and he had a chance to hear them, that he would make his decision.

When Sharon Matusik became the Dean at the University of Colorado's Leeds School of Business, she wanted to figure out how to make the graduates more employable. So she went on a listening tour of Colorado businesses. She asked founders and members of the C-suite in start-up and Fortune 1000 companies, "What is the future of business, and what does it take to lead in your sector?" Not surprisingly, many of the key themes were things that comedians do well: communication skills, critical thinking, grit and resilience, learning from experience, and...collaboration.

Matusik returned to campus with the goal to incorporate these kinds of skills into a curriculum focused on experiential learning.

Listening goes a long way for well-established businesses too. Many times product lines are so mature that companies can't find new customers, so they seek out feedback from existing customers about ways they can serve them better. The typical way to do this is with a focus group of a few diehard customers. But there is a wealth of data that companies can mine for good ideas. Amazon reviews—where customers share the good, the bad, and the ugly—have become one such place.

Some products have such high market penetration that anyone who needs it has it. In the case of tin foil, for example, it's not a matter of getting people to start using the product; it's a matter of getting them to use *more* of it, in new ways. For example, Arm & Hammer relies on its customers to execute this strategy for its baking soda. To celebrate their customers' ingenuity, the company launched "More Power To You," which invited customers to submit a novel use of the product along with a reenactment of the Arm & Hammer Baking Soda logo (an "arm flex"). People sent in a wide range of new uses, including "Glow Slime Soda, inspired by Annabelle," "Dino Eggs Soda, inspired by Ava," and "Double Your Stash, inspired by Walter White."

Kidding. Heisenberg would never cut his drugs.

COMPLEMENTATION

Having a team that actively supports and listens is amazing, but it's important to take a step back and look at who the team is made of—does the team have the essential skills that it needs to be successful?

The three major jobs of a CEO: 1) make big, bold predictions about where the company needs to go (strategy); 2) hire the right people and set the mindset of the company (culture); 3) find the capital to execute strategy and implement culture (finance).

When creating culture, founders, CEO's, and middle-managers lean toward hiring people like themselves because it is easy to get along. Unfortunately, that doesn't maximize results. In the world of comedy and business, diversity is critically important. Being different creates the possibility for complementation. Complementation is the magic made when opposites come together, creating a sum that is greater than its parts.

Lorne Michaels, creator of *Saturday Night Live,* actively seeks complementation. In her memoir *Bossypants*, Tina Fey describes the way that Michaels builds a writer's room. By bringing together the Harvard Lampoon comedians (heady, esoteric, joke-writing types) with the more Chicago, blue collar-style comedians (better storytellers), he gets a much better product with wider appeal.

A PIRATE, A ROBOT, AND A NINJA WALK INTO A BAR...

Upright Citizen's Brigade improviser and teacher Billy Merritt created a taxonomy of improv styles called Pirate Robot Ninja. Then he and Will Hines (the "listening" guy) wrote the book *Pirate Robot Ninja: An Improv Fable.*

According to Merritt, Pirates are fearless. "They get out there first, they provide the wind for the sails, and they provide the energy."

Will Hines says that Melissa McCarthy is a pirate:

> She's impulsive, energetic, fun, mischievous, dangerous, and brash. Who knows what her actual internal process is, but that's the energy she gives off. She seems like someone who would fearlessly jump into a situation and improvise her way out. That's a pirate.

Robots, on the other hand, are more, well, mechanical. Merritt explains it this way:

> The robot analyzes things and decides this is what needs to be done. A robot sees the pattern and creates the pattern, makes the connections, adds all the color for the scene, and makes it work. The straight men, if you will, the voice of reason, the justifier.

Will Hines says that Anthony Jeselnik is robot-like:

> Stand-ups tend to be robots. The thinkers, the writers, they want to know the rules. They want to know before they take a step. They want to know how it's going to pay off at the end, but they're also good at remembering everything, giving things a purpose, finding patterns and labeling what's going on. They tend to be observers.

If you have an improv group of all pirates, it's a mess. Merritt says a team comprised only of pirates is equivalent to "a bunch of tornadoes on stage." They don't have great memories, and the scene will undoubtedly go off course. But if you have an improv group of all robots, the scene won't pop. You need both.

The next level is the Ninja—a person who has mastered both roles and can fill whatever role is missing.

Merritt recommends finding out if you are a pirate or a robot. "Are you more impulsive? Are you more analytical? Own it. Work on your other side until you find balance, and then become the ninja, the ultimate improviser."

CREATING COMPLEMENTATION IN COMEDY

Chappelle's Show benefitted from the complementation of Dave Chappelle and Neal Brennan. Having a multi-racial co-creator team allowed them to tackle race relations in a groundbreaking way. And they had the dynamic Pirate (Chappelle) and Robot (Brennan) duo happening, too.

A dynamic duo appears in the modern-day double act performance that originated in American Vaudeville and British music halls. It features two performers—a "straight" and a "clown"—who have so much contrast that they generate the premise for all sorts of comedic interactions.

This contrasting duo appears in other cultures as well. The backbone of Japanese comedy is *manzai*—the equivalent to the double act. In *manzai*, the two-man comedy style comprised of the straight partner, or *tsukkomi*, trading gags with and smacking around a *boke*, the goofball partner. In China, the traditional comedic performance *xiangsheng,* or crosstalk, is more common than stand-up. There is a dialogue between two performers.

Some of the most famous comedy double acts through the years include:

- Lucy and Ricky
- Laurel and Hardy
- Abbott and Costello
- Martin and Lewis
- Laverne and Shirley

- Jay and Silent Bob
- Mauss and McGraw

COMPLEMENTATION IN COMMERCE

The Lorne Michaels approach to the writer's room is equally important in business, from the smallest startup to the biggest Fortune 500 company. The research on the benefits of a diverse workforce is overwhelming. A variety of perspectives and personality styles lead to better problem solving and enhanced creativity.

Shane Snow, the author of *Dream Teams*, says it well: "Two heads are better than one, if they see things differently."

Anita Woolley, an organizational behavior professor at Carnegie Mellon University, has done some fascinating work on how to create high-functioning teams in the workplace.[29] The conventional thinking is that the way to make smarter teams is to fill them with smarter workers. The key criterion is the general intelligence (called G in the research world) of each worker. Hire the best, and together they'll be a super-team.

What Woolley's lab found, however, contradicts that

---

29 Woolley, A.W., Chabris, C.F., Pentland, A., Hashmi, N. & Malone, T.M. (2010). Evidence for a collective intelligence factor in the performance of human groups, *Science*, 330, 686-688.

conventional wisdom. Teams made up of "crazy smart" people don't always perform the best. The individual intelligence G of each team member wasn't the best predictor of team success. As it turns out, it's not only people's individual attributes that are important, but also how well they work together. Woolley found that C—the Collective Intelligence of the team—was a better predictor of how well the team performed than the sum of G—the individual intelligence of team members. A team with all smart people (people with high G) can make teams too one-dimensional. And teams that are too one-dimensional don't always perform the best.

Her research finds that teams with more women than men perform above average due to the need for social perceptiveness in team dynamics, which women typically do better than men. However, this performance improvement shows up mainly when introducing women to all-male teams. When a team is all women, the performance levels off. All of one type is bad.

If you only look to hire the same people based on the same criterion—even if that criterion is intelligence—you can end up with a one-dimensional team. That might work if business was like baseball, where the players act more or less on an individual basis and you just add up their performance. In that case you would want to pay top dollar to acquire every superstar you could and assemble a 'dream team.'

But business isn't like baseball. It's more like basketball, where it helps for everyone to touch the ball—even though one person ends up shooting it.

WOULD YOU LIKE TO DANCE?

With 267,000 employees worldwide, Pepsi is one of the most diverse workplaces in the world. Many would assume that the company would be good at understanding how to connect to a diverse population. Yet their commercial with supermodel Kendall Jenner suggests that an attractive light-skinned woman sharing a soda with a police officer can solve race relations and police brutality. Widely criticized as tone-deaf, critics rightfully asked, "How did this commercial get approved?" Pepsi needed to get more feedback from a more diverse audience—they needed to listen.

Diversity is clearly required for complementation, but it's important not to stop at diversity. In order to reap the benefits of diversity, this is another crucial step: inclusion. But inclusivity is often overlooked, as my University of Colorado colleague Stefanie Johnson has studied, which can steer even the most diverse workplaces toward failure.

Diversity is the result of hiring decisions, but inclusion is the result of culture. Successful businesses listen to their employees, especially if they disagree or have critical feedback. While "willingness to give feedback," "openness," and "honesty" could be traits that you hire for, a better way is to bake these mindsets into a company's culture. This is what academics call psychological safety.

But if employees believe they won't be heard or are afraid of being punished for saying something unpopular, they won't speak up. And then you don't have inclusion.

Remember, company culture starts with the CEO. It is important to encourage feedback and express gratitude when others disagree. Don't confuse this with being simply polite. There should be candor without consequences.

Verna Myers, VP of Inclusion Strategy at Netflix, says it best:

> Diversity is being invited to the party. Inclusion is being asked to dance.

True inclusion is diversity + support + listening. And inclusion is the key to complementation.

Animated Inclusion

Making a movie is difficult. Filmmakers seek to stir emotions, present pleasing aesthetic experiences, and create compelling plots. *Everything* needs to go well and rarely does that happen. Yet Pixar has had hit after hit after hit, from *Toy Story* to *Finding Nemo* to *Coco*. Pixar's brain trust has been very thoughtful about creating psychological safety in their company, fostering a place that is not open to bullying and incivility. Without this kind of environment, the critical first in the Pixar process—revising early versions of the films and giving notes—would not be possible. Anyone in the company can give feedback, from a voice actor to a janitor.

The freedom to share your thoughts and opinions about the work, without shame or fear of repercussions, is what makes all the difference for people to do their best work.

Healthy Inclusion

Another company modeling diversity *and* inclusivity is Medtronic. A global company with offices on four continents and headquartered in Minneapolis, they invented medical devices such as pacemakers and insulin pumps. While this may sound like a company run by robots, it is all about humans.

I spoke to Kamrin Helland, the director of global marketing, about how the company pursues diversity. They conduct the typical practices of seeking candidates from diverse backgrounds. And supporting employees is one of the six tenants from the company's original mission statement.

But where the company stands out is inclusivity, especially in the way they listen to their customers. For example, the company regularly conducts engagement surveys in order to identify potential problems. It gets interesting after a problem is identified. Rather than having the leadership team say how to fix the problem, the company creates "culture circles" in order to identify ways to solve it. Moreover, Medtronic allows employees to form grassroots resource groups based on culture, ethnicity, faith, sexual orientation, disability, and veteran status.

Besides crushing it financially, Medtronic was on the "World's 25 Best Multinational Workplaces" list by Great Place to Work Institute.

IMPLICATION: THE MASTER OF ENERGY

Complementation doesn't just happen. It's the coming together of specific skills in a specific way so they can function at their best. Each piece supports the others so that the sum is greater than its parts.

Failing at complementation can lead to self-sabotage. For instance, when a company has a big thorny problem to solve, it assembles smart people (hopefully with diverse perspectives) to work together to solve it.

Meet Ethan Decker, president of Applied Brand Science.

In his previous life in the advertising world, he was often asked to MC problem-solving sessions like these. As a skilled facilitator and moderator, he's good at creating exercises and workshops to solve business problems. Often this group of talented people is put into a corporate-looking room with stiff office chairs around a rectangular table, under bright fluorescent lights. There's little to no art on the walls (to allow space for dry erase boards and sticky notes). There's no natural light—either there are no windows out to the world, or the blinds are drawn so people can see the slide presentation better on the screen. And there's very little in the way of food or drinks or sustenance. Then the group is asked to think freely and be vulnerable and collaborate to come up with brilliant solutions.

Decker has been at far too many of these meetings, and so have you. Nowadays, he sees his first job as creating a better environment for opening people up to collaboration.

He opens blinds to let in natural light. He hands out water and other drinks. He puts out healthy snacks. He encourages people to get up and move around. He brings jackets, and even blankets or pashminas, in case the temperature is too cold for anyone. (Office temperatures are typically set to accommodate men, who tend to run "warmer" than women and who often wear more layers at work. Like wool suits. And sweater vests.) He turns on music during breaks—not just to lift the mood, but to invite conversation: music provides some ambient noise so that people having side conversations have a little privacy. And while people are chatting or humming to the music, he cleans up the room so that it feels less like a dorm after a party.

All of Decker's actions create a context where the group assembled can be their most productive selves. His attentiveness to creating a context where his team can thrive is a great example of servant leadership. He cares as much about the energy in the room as the content they need to cover.

He transforms himself from the MC (the master of ceremonies) to The Master of Energy.

DEVELOP YOUR SHTICK

Here are some ways you can improve your cooperation.

BUILD YOUR TEAM

Remember, there is no such thing as a lone genius. You

need the genius of others, and the act of cooperating to innovate starts at the top. Leaders must gather the right people and support them to be their best. Only then can you truly make something epic.

Identify who you need to succeed. Ask yourself:

- Am I a pirate or a robot? From there, you can recognize your deficiencies and try to improve them. You can also intentionally seek out your ideal complementary team members.
- Who is my Merrill Markoe? Or who is my David Letterman?
- Is there a toxic worker on your team? Who is it? If you can't figure out, dare to ask: *Is it me?*

Remember the benefit of diversity only happens when you have inclusivity. Be inclusive.

BE A BETTER TEAMMATE

In the context of your career, listening is difficult for a couple of reasons. First, nearly everyone wants to look smart in a meeting. The impulse is to jump straight in and present "the answer." It feels good to show off and be the one with the solution. If you hang back and listen first, someone else might get all the glory. And when you've presented a solution, you don't want to hear any naysayers, so you don't listen to feedback. Someone might disagree with you, and you might have to change your mind.

Be honest: How good are you listening skills? Use the following scale:

___ Okay. ___ Bad. ___ Terrible. ___ Terribly awfully bad. ___ What did you say?

What if you plan your listening with the same intention as you plan what you say?

- In a meeting, ask yourself: can I wait for everyone else to talk?
- Make a plan not to add your input until _____ happens
- When networking, think of it like being at a party where you are meeting interesting people.
- Become a Master of Energy: show up early, prep the room, and bring dark chocolate.

Remember that the benefit of diversity only happens when you have inclusivity. Be inclusive. (Yes, this line is listed twice. It's that important. Let's say it one more time just for fun: *Remember the benefit of diversity only happens when you have inclusivity.*)

WALK THE TIGHT ROPE

As a reader, you might notice the paradox that I am creating: Destroy the status quo and take no prisoners! Cooperate with others to execute and innovate! Because both are true—and if you can tap into both, you will be unstoppable.

In either case, the common denominator in your career (and life) is you. More than talent, it is your intentional work ethic that will make the difference. In the coming chapters we will shift focus to specific behaviors that you as an individual can act out, behaviors that directly impact which rung you reach on your chosen ladder of success.

ACT OUT: SUCCESS BY 1,000 CUTS

The epitome of the lean startup is Vaudeville. Comedians would test their jokes, dump the ones that didn't work, and improve the ones that did. Modern stand-ups do the same thing. They fail fast. They release their earliest prototypes to their target audience, get feedback, and iterate for improvements.

SET THE BAR LOW

Failures are good, but failures should be low stakes. Comedians never try a new joke while filming a comedy special. By the time they hit the big stage with six cameras rolling, they already know what jokes work and what jokes don't. That includes crowd work, which, though it's improvised, is thoroughly explored and intensely practiced.

When Jay Leno was doing *The Tonight Show*, he would go to the Comedy and Magic Club in Hermosa Beach every Sunday night and do a set. He'd stand at the mic with note cards and try out jokes that he would use for his monologue that coming week. Jokes that were good were more likely to end up on the air. The jokes that weren't, he would either revise or kill.

Starting with a proof of concept helps you test ideas to

ensure they are on the right track, before investing gobs of time and money and energy. The premise for the show *It's Always Sunny in Philadelphia* came from a scene shot on a crappy camera in an apartment. It cost $85.

FAILURE TO TEST, FAILURE TO LAUNCH

Unfortunately, too many businesses don't bother to test while the stakes are small. The result is that when they fail, they often fail big. CEOs cite the famous quote by Henry Ford as their permission. "If I had asked people what they wanted, they would have said a faster horse." Though this quote is his most famous, they might want to adjust their thinking. There's no evidence Ford ever said it.[30]

CEOs also cite Apple's success launching disruptive products. Like Ford, Steve Jobs is lauded as someone who doesn't listen to his audience; he leads them. He's often quoted as saying, "It's really hard to design products by focus groups. A lot of times, people don't know what they want until you show it to them." And he was somehow able to hide the development of the iPod, iPad, and iPhone before revealing them in big, splashy launches.

---

30 Ford also is attributed another quote about the Model T that shows he wasn't as customer-centric as subsequent car manufactures, "Any customer can have a car painted any color that he wants so long as it is black."

However, Apple and Ford are the exceptions that prove the rule. There are just as many instances of splashy launch failures (e.g., Segway, One Laptop Per Child) as there are successes. For example, Google hid away its "game-changing" Google Glass and never fully tested with the kinds of people it affected. So when they released it to the world in 2014, it was a spectacular flop. It wasn't that the technology didn't work; it's that no one liked it. The product, which augmented reality and allowed users to interface with the internet through a pair of eyeglasses, turned out to be appalling in two ways: first as a fashion statement, with wearers affectionately known as "glass-holes", and second, as a privacy concern—no one wants to be unknowingly videotaped.

CEOs and other managers misinterpret the Henry Ford quote. Customers will indicate the need that needs to be satisfied. In Ford's day, people wanted to get from place A to place B *faster*. It was up to the entrepreneur to figure out how to make a car instead of a horse.

And like Ford's quote, there's much more to the story with Steve Jobs and Apple. A lawsuit between Samsung and Apple revealed that Apple conducted tons of market research to better understand their audience, their competition, and their market. True, Jobs didn't just do what customers asked them to do. But he would listen to their frustrations with current options, and then invent solutions to them.

Who Moved My Orange Juice?

Here's another shocking story about the importance of testing in the marketplace. In 2009, Tropicana wanted to update their packaging. They hired a famous designer from New York, the kind of man who wears an ascot and references Leonardo Da Vinci when talking about soda cans. The new design was radical. It replaced the product's well-known imagery ("Tropicana" in bold font and a straw stuck in a juicy orange). Gone was the orange and the logo was turned sideways in a new font.

The new packaging was announced with great fanfare to the press. And it was accompanied by an expensive ad campaign. But when the new packages hit the shelves, sales dropped 20 percent.

Remember Ethan Decker, our master of energy and president of Applied Brand Science? He claims that market research may have both caused the issue and helped avoid it.

As a billion-dollar brand, it's unlikely that Tropicana skipped the critical stage of market research that's often built into a big company's packaging processes. They probably showed concepts to focus groups and asked online panels of consumers to gauge their "purchase intent" for the new designs. Decker speculates that people would have indeed rated the new packaging as "new," "fresh," or "modern" compared to the old design.

Decker attributes the Tropicana loss not to consumers hating the design, but because it camouflaged a familiar product in a shelf full of juice. "No one recognized it anymore. They'd stroll down the aisle with their shopping cart, not see their usual brand, assume it wasn't stocked, and buy a different brand. In fact many people said the brand looked like a private label brand, a store brand." Decker believes they probably didn't test the new packaging on the shelves, in a shopping situation, where people are simply trying to *find* the brand, not ponder whether it's new and modern.

Seven weeks later the company returned to the old packaging—at a price tag of $35 million.

An agile mindset requires listening to customers early and often. While all this might make perfect sense for the start-up phase, growing businesses often stop embracing innovation and small, calculated failures after they've become well-established. They feel like they have too much to lose. So they play it safe. Or so they think.

SHTICK FROM SHANE

There is a saying in comedy: *Stage time. Stage time. Stage time.* Get on stage as often as possible to practice. But really, it's not just stage time. It's the opportunity to test new, raw material and get feedback. It's an opportunity to take chances.

But often, when a comic does find success, they stop taking the very chances that made them successful and instead go with what they know. The goal is no longer to create something new and fresh, but to avoid failure at all costs.

My own career is a prime example of exactly how this can happen. When I started out in open mics and then doing regular club spots, I was fearless. I took massive swings at comedy that often struck out on stage. But because of this, I was hitting home runs too. And home runs are what people get excited about, so when you are hitting them, they even respect the strikeouts. Even when they didn't, most gigs don't really matter anyway. If you bomb at a one-time show for the Elks Lodge, then who cares? It's all just practice for the big game.

But once that practice pays off and you become a full-time, headlining comedian, things change. Headlining a show, you aren't allowed to fail as much. You need to get rebooked back at this club and get referrals from them for other shows. You can no longer alienate an audience and laugh about it after. This is your livelihood. People paid good money to be entertained and you are the main event. You can't just perform to make your comic friends in the back of the room laugh. They don't pay your rent.

And because of this, you stop taking the chances and stick with the material you know works. You don't need to break ground, and if you try to, you'll probably fall in. Instead, you just want to be reliable.

But the problem is, if you don't keep finding ways to take chances, you will plateau and quickly fade into the collection of once-promising comedians who are now stuck on the road just trying to get by. And even if you're making rent, it takes a toll on your soul. We can't let our routine become routine.

This is exactly what happened to me.

To get out of it, I eventually had to change almost everything that I was doing. I needed to reinvent myself (a couple of times). I found smaller, more experimental places that paid less reliably. It breathed new life into my stale career. Now I look back at the comfortable existence of being a comedy club headliner as something that was suffocating my career. I'm not made for getting walked to first base. I'm made for swinging for the fences.

For example, I don't even know if that was an accurate baseball reference, but I took a chance anyway and nailed it! TOUCHDOWN!!!

CHAPTER 5

WRITE IT OR REGRET IT

Janeane Garofalo is a versatile comedian. She has done sketch comedy on *Saturday Night Live*. She's starred in movies such as *Reality Bites* and TV shows such as *The Larry Sanders Show*. She's been a radio host for *Air America*, and she even wrote a book, *Feel This Book*, with Ben Stiller. But throughout her tour de force of the comedy world, the consistent thread has been her stand-up.

You may not have realized that Garofalo is part of a comedy duo—with her notebook. She relies on it so much that she unashamedly brings it with her on stage. She's also not afraid to talk about it. From her self-titled 1997 TV comedy special:

The notebook. Yes, as you know, Garofalo's a little forgetful. Has to bring her notebook. Between the NutraSweet and the Fen-phen, I don't know whether to sh*t or wind my watch at this point. I gotta have a thing happening here because I don't wanna forget what I wanna discuss with you. I owe you that much.

No matter your industry, field, or expertise, there is one essential habit everyone should have. From capturing creativity to executing innovation, it all requires this simple yet all-too-often overlooked step: *write it down.*

WRITE THIS WAY

People tend to think of comedians as performers. Or degenerates. But really, 68 percent of the comedic brilliance is the outcome of writing as a craft. I want you to start thinking about writing the way that comedians think about writing.

Stand-up comedians are either writers who must invent themselves as performers (e.g., Seinfeld), or performers who must invent themselves as writers (e.g., Chappelle).

There are, of course, exceptions. For example, Mitch Hedberg was such a good writer that he could afford to not be a good performer. He would perform with his eyes closed, his back to the audience, with sungla⸴ his hair in front of his face. If it was up to hi curl up into the fetal position with his mic⸴⸴ read his jokes.

Along with writers and performers, there are two other categories of people in comedy: people who want to do comedy, and people who want to get paid.

For the latter, being a comedy writer in Hollywood is steady work and it pays relatively well. Many comedians write material and perform on stage in order to get a writing job.

If you need evidence of how important writing is, just look at the 2007 Hollywood writer's strike. Without writers, the entertainment industry ground to a halt. Late night talk shows moved to reruns, and most scripted television programs either had their seasons shortened or canceled. This is why the Writer's Guild is the most powerful union in Hollywood. We think of Hollywood as these beautiful people on screen and amazing special effects. But those things don't matter if you don't have great stories. And for that, you need not-so-beautiful writers sitting around a rectangular table downing La Croix and riffing off each other for hours. If screen actors went on strike, they would be easier to replace than the writers. Well, except for Brad Pitt.

We often think of writing as a means of communicating to others. Like comedy, it requires an audience. This is true, but sometimes the audience is *you*. Writing can be as much about clarifying your thoughts and ideas for yourself as it can be about communicating those thoughts and ideas to others.

Like a yoga practice, creating a writing practice that is just for you brings benefits to both your personal and professional life. And from this solid foundation, you can level up your ideas for the world.

THE MIGHTY PEN

Oh, what's that? You're not a writer? Can't write? Don't like to write? Well suck it up. I had the same problem.

As a young man, I thought I could have a career as a professor, but I was too naïve to realize my chances were slim. I was a good enough student to believe I had a shot at getting into a top PhD program. But these programs typically take students with near-perfect GPAs and near-perfect GRE scores. I had neither.

After four years of trying, more than thirty applications, and thousands of hours of extra study, one university decided to take a chance on me. Thank you, Ohio State

University. Actually, it was one *person* who took a chance on me. Thank you, Barb Mellers.[31]

Ten years later I was an assistant professor at the University of Colorado's Leeds School of Business. I was facing a tenure decision (in other words, I was up for a promotion). And I had a huge hole in my skillset: writing.

As a researcher in academia, long-term rewards (i.e., tenure) come from being a Principal Investigator, or lead researcher, who leads projects that result in academic papers. A key skill is to write precisely, write persuasively, and publish frequently.[32] Up to that point, I had been successful by assisting my fabulous co-authors. I would spend ten to twelve hours a day in the lab doing the things I was good at: creating experiments and analyzing data.

I loved my job, and I didn't want the school to get rid of me. So I took a cold, hard look at myself and faced facts: I wasn't good at writing. But I knew I had to *get* good at

---

31 I found out after I arrived in my PhD program how I got in. I had applied to the social psychology program, and unbeknownst to me, that had been summarily rejected. Barb was a new faculty member in the quantitative psychology program and was eager to build a lab with students interested in emotions and decision-making. Not satisfied with the crop of applicants, she walked down the hallway and got the "reject pile" from the admin. She looked through and pulled out an application—my application—and took a chance on me. True story.

32 There is a non-funny quip in the academy that PhD stands for "pile it high and deep."

writing. So I got my butt in the chair and started writing. A lot.

Becoming a regular writer saved my career. And when I say "regular," I mean "daily."

Not only did the quantity of my production go up (i.e., I published more), but the quality of my research went up. This is because I was writing early and often. It forced me to get much more precise about what it is that I was talking about. And I got better at answering the scientific questions I was needed to answer. I was promoted with tenure, and now my peers are stuck with me.

Writing is one reason I succeeded. Comedy is the other reason. As I began to study humor (through writing) and uncover all these insights about how comedy applies to business (through writing), my ideas developed clearly enough that I was able to apply them to my career and achieved astounding results.

To show you what I mean, let's look at three reasons to write: to remember, to clarify, and to communicate.

WRITE TO REMEMBER

A notebook, not a microphone, is the most critical tool for the masters of comedy.

Many episodes of *Seinfeld* are based on a premise from Larry David's notebook which he wrote years earlier.

David Sedaris, renowned humor and memoir writer, needs to write down everything he sees and does in a journal. He has kept every single journal since age thirteen, some of which he uses as source material for his comedy. He even turns them into books.

The sooner you start writing, the sooner you begin capturing the building blocks of your future. But beware, there's a legacy of writers losing their notebooks.

Kevin Smith had all his notes for his breakout movie *Clerks* in a trash bag in his car. His car got broken into and he lost the bag.

Mitch Hedberg lost his notebook, and it's the only time his wife Lynn Shawcroft ever saw him cry.

Janeane Garofalo got mugged and her notebook was stolen. She has a joke about it:

> I got mugged. And they got my knapsack with my comedy notebook in it. So if anybody sees two cholos bombing at the Funny Bone chain, that would be them. Just give me a jingle.

In a "woke" world, I am not sure we are allowed to say

cholo anymore. Nevertheless, losing a notebook may not matter as much as these comedians suggest. Yes, we write things down so we don't have to remember them, but the act of writing them down actually helps you remember it.

Research reveals the benefits of writing with pen and paper. It forces you to slow down your thinking and increases your memory of the material. Some professors are banning laptops during lectures because of the evidence in favor of handwritten notes. If it's a choice between typing it up or not writing it down, then by all means, type it. But be aware that phone and laptop are also horrific forms of distraction.

So chances are that if you've written it down, you'll remember it. But if you don't write it down in the first place...you've already lost it.

LET'S GET APPLICABLE

Writing things down has powerful results.

Joan Rivers kept all of her jokes—too many to count—on index cards in a set of files. The toughest part of dealing with the library-esque card catalog was deciding what category to put a joke in. No Boolean word searches were available in her Upper East Side apartment in New York City.

SHTICK FROM SHANE

I used to have a note pad *and* a voice recorder that I used religiously to capture ideas. If I didn't write down an idea, I felt like it was throwing money on the ground.

Jokes are my currency.

Like many comics, I now capture my ideas on my phone. There are some advantages. The ideas are easy to edit, they're searchable, they're easy to read (i.e., no terrible handwriting), and they're backed up to the cloud. But I am reconsidering my practice.

When I carry around a notepad, I am more mindful of joke opportunities. You know the old saying, "When you have a hammer, everything looks like a nail." Well, when you have a notepad, everything looks like a joke.

PS: This is also why I don't carry a gun.

You can use writing to remind you of what you want and inspire you to go after it. When Steve Harvey was a boy, his teacher gave him an assignment to write down what he wanted to be when he grew up. Harvey said he was going to be on television. His teacher told him to pick something realistic that he could actually accomplish. Distressed, he went home and talked to his dad. His dad told him to write something that would make the teacher happy, but encouraged him to stick with his dreams of TV stardom.

Harvey completed the assignment, before penning a personal manifesto about his goal to be on television. He read it every night. And, of course, later in life he did get on TV—most famously hosting *Family Feud*. After fulfilling his goals in his manifesto, Harvey sent that teacher a brand-new television set. And he didn't stop. He continued to send her a new TV each year after.[33] At some point she told him, "You need to stop sending me television sets because my house is now filled with television sets!" Besides not being the world's most encouraging teacher, she couldn't figure out how to use eBay.

People have a tendency to be very good about remembering the things we're right about and bad about remembering the things we're not right about. So writing ideas down can actually improve our learning. It gives you this honest record that shows what you believed earlier, which may or may not prove to be correct as time passes. Management guru Peter Drucker would write down what he expected to happen and then come back and write down what actually happened. This helped him learn from mistakes, hone his instincts, and plan for the future. Journaling is useful for us mere mortals in the same way.

And if you need any more proof of the power of writing

---

33 Kevin Hart once sent an $8,000 bottle of wine to someone who gave him a poor review.

things down: Einstein is famous for writing a handful of academic papers, but he made 80,000 pages of notes.

WRITE TO CLARIFY

Recording to remember is like dumping ideas on a page. It's crappy first drafts and aimless journaling. But writing can also help with clarity. Writing exposes weakness in thought and reason. Writing helps you to workshop an idea. The precision that is necessary when writing down words and ideas demands a level of clarity. It slows you down and makes you acknowledge what you don't know.

Darwyn Metzger is the founder and CEO of Phantom, an advertising, branding, and marketing firm that specializes as a business accelerator. He is so good at what he does that all of his work comes from referrals. Consequently, his firm went years without even having a website. Metzger is out-of-this-world creative. Not surprisingly, I met him in an improv class while researching my first book.

I invited him to give a guest lecture to my MBAs. This is somewhat ironic: he's an MBA program dropout. I often start class by discussing current events related to marketing. Normally when I have a guest speaker, they use this time to review their notes or scroll through their phone.

Not Metzger. Instead, he furiously scribbled in his yellow

legal pad. After I introduced him, he said, "Thank you very much. Before I begin, I'd like to comment on your current events." He went on to make numerous observations that no one else had come up with (over fifty students in the class), demonstrating his wide-ranging knowledge of business, art, technology, finance, and cryptocurrency.

It was his ability to write *and* to hone his ideas in the moment that allowed him to contribute to the class in breathtaking fashion.

IF IT DOESN'T FIT, YOU MUST QUIT

The value of writing to clarify applies especially well to business planning. Gone are the days of long business and marketing plans. Things are fast and lean—or ought to be. That leads us to the beauty of the one-pager (aka the one-sheet).

Whenever I talk to people contemplating any creative endeavor (business or otherwise), I ask them if they've written their one-pager. Some of them say, "No, not yet." Others say, "What's a one-pager?"

A one-pager is exactly what it sounds like. I learned about the one-pager late in my career when my co-author and I began to write *The Humor Code*. We took six weeks to write the one-pager, and after that, we only needed three weeks to write the book proposal. And when you look at the one-pager and the book, it is amazing how close they feel.

A one-pager includes an attention-getting lead description that identifies who your idea is for, what it does, and how it's different. You must revise, revise, revise, revise, revise, revise, revise, revise, and revise. You can't be sloppy with your thoughts. Because. It. Must. Fit. On. One. Page.

Every potential project I do (and every major project I don't do) has a one-pager, including this one. I need the one-pager to figure out if the project is worth doing. When I'm finished, I often decide, "Nope. I'm not going to do this project." If I decide, "Oh this needs to happen yesterday," then my one-pager shifts from clarification to communication.[34]

Amazon has a conceptually similar practice when contemplating a new product. Before management can decide to take on any new project, the person spearheading the project must write the press release. The press release must be consumer-centric and feel newsworthy and important to the target customers. This helps the team probe how customers would think and feel about the product or service before they even begin creating it.

---

34 *The Humor Code* one-pager and the one-pager for this book are in the workbook that you can download from my webpage.

Amazon has another writing process for new projects: the six-page memo. This process not only clarifies the idea and communicates to the team what is required, but it cuts back on meetings, because everything they've thought of has been documented in a clear and meaningful way. The first thing they do is give everyone time (up to an hour) to read the memo.

WRITE TO COMMUNICATE

Once your idea is developed, your writing moves from an internal document to become an external document.

When you're writing to communicate, you are not writing for yourself anymore. You are writing for others. They simply do not care about your message as much as you. They also don't know your message to begin with.

When it comes to communication, people struggle with the curse of knowledge. How is that a problem? When someone knows everything about a topic, they don't realize what their audience doesn't know, so they leave out important information that would bridge the gap. The solution for this is to first identify the *singular important idea* you're trying to communicate. Then determine the necessary prerequisites to understanding that idea. Finally, ensure that those prerequisites are addressed in some way in your communication.

WRITE FAT, GET SKINNY

Recording to remember is all about quantity. It's writing fat. Your job is just to get it down. As you clarify, you continue to add more fat, but in specific places, until you have everything you need. Editing is about trimming the fat, but keeping the meat.

A problem writers have is that they are overly wordy—failing to capture the *essence* of what they're trying to say.

You must strip away the non-essential. This is the art of editing.

Editing is obviously a big part of comedy. As Shakespeare wrote, "As are your words more briefly and expertly expressed, incised of droll baggage and heft, so does your quotient of wit and wisdom increase."

Kidding. He wrote, "Brevity is the soul of wit."

When writing jokes, shorter is almost always better. The masters of editing are one-liner comedians such as Henny Youngman. Comedians will compete to see who can create the shortest joke. Norm Macdonald thinks the perfect joke is when the setup and punchline are identical.

Mitch Hedberg has a funny five-word joke:

I think Big Foot is blurry.

Not to be outdone, Jimmy Carr has a four-word joke:

Venison's dear isn't it?

Carr has a two-word joke too, but it can't be repeated here.

One tool for getting skinny is to create a constraint. I favor the 10 percent rule. If I have a piece of writing that I feel pretty comfortable with, I then look to eliminate 10 percent of the words. The goal is, obviously, not to sacrifice any of the meaning or the ideas, but to find the fat I originally refused to see.

SHTICK FROM SHANE

Hemmingway is believed to have said, "Write drunk and edit sober." My variant is write long and speak short.

I just write to be writing. I don't write to be funny. I don't write to be good. But what happens is that a single line will pop off the page that grabs my attention. That is the tiny idea that turns into a one-liner.

PS: I wrote this while drunk and edited it on Adderall.

LEVERAGING BREVITY

When working on *The Humor Code*, I teamed up with my colleague Phil Fernbach to conduct an analysis of *The New Yorker* cartoon caption contest. In this contest, the magazine publishes a captionless cartoon, and thousands of readers submit captions that they believe make the drawing funnier. Cartoon editor Bob Mankoff would make a short list of the most promising captions, and then chose the best three for readers to vote on.

One factor that Fernbach and I examined was the length of the submitted captions. It turns out the shortlisted captions were shorter by one word on average than the rejected ones. That doesn't sound like a lot, but the captions were only 9-10 words on average.

Contest 281 was won by Roger Ebert, who, along with being a renowned movie critic, was a regular caption contest player. The cartoon is of a couple carrying shopping bags, apparently looking for their car, who have ended up in a vast desert. They come across a parking lot signpost with a large letter "F". The winning caption: "I'm not going to say the word I'm thinking of."

NEARLY EVERYTHING IS TOO LONG

When people complain about an experience—a comedy set, a movie, a novel, a lecture—they almost never say,

"That wasn't long enough." Instead they say, "Could have cut ten minutes off that movie," or, "You know, there were a bunch of jokes that he told that weren't very funny."

Why does that happen?

Let's walk through it. The process of making an experience usually occurs in a create-then-cut sequence. Say you're making a film. You shoot all the footage, arrange it into a rough cut that's five to seven hours long, and then you trim the fat down to a mere 120 minutes. But it probably only needs to be 110 minutes. Think they'll cut it down that far? Not likely.

When you're looking at a cut/no-cut decision, there's both a potential loss (of not being able to use it) alongside the gain (the benefit of not having it), but since losses loom larger than gains in our minds, people tend to leave things in more often than they should.

This is compounded by the sunk cost fallacy; that is, people are reluctant to give up the time, effort, or money that went into creating these things. A comedian might work on a joke for months and, even if it's not as strong as it should be, they leave it in because it's too painful to cut. They'd have to emotionally write off the sunk costs into the making of that joke.

The third reason is ego. You think that it's brilliant or hilarious, even if no one else thinks it is. Being in love with a joke is one of the worst things that a comedian can do because it doesn't matter if the person who's delivering the joke likes it; it matters if the audience does.

As a writer, your words are like your children, your darlings. But as the saying goes, "Kill your darlings."

Ego makes it hard to remove those darlings. And if *nearly everything is too long*, this means that *nearly everything could be better*. The mixture of loss aversion, sunk cost, and egotism convinces entertainers to leave in jokes, scenes, and sentences that don't actually serve the audience.[35]

And audiences notice the bad things more than they notice the good things. Time may fly when you're having fun, but it slows down when you're not. So if you fail to cut and instead leave in things the audience won't enjoy—unfunny jokes, boring scenes, and bad special effects—the audience cannot help but notice them. The negative aspects of the experience overshadow the positive, making it feel like nearly everything is too long.

So the solution? Cut the unnecessary, no matter the cost. Cut till it hurts.

---

35 You probably noticed that in chapter two. My apologies.

Now this might sound contradictory to what I said previously about writing jokes that you love, first and foremost, but it's not. You should write whatever you love first, then test it—with your target audience. If it doesn't land, change it. If it still doesn't land, cut it. This is the painful beauty of creating—managing the tight-rope tension between what you love and what gets results.

IMPLICATION: SUBTRACT. SUBTRACT. SUBTRACT.

The lesson of making deep cuts in order to improve a message—and the risk of not cutting something that needs to go—applies to a wide array of non-writing decisions, professional or otherwise. Bear with me as I apply a writing lesson to product design more generally.

Our natural tendency is to add things when we want to make them better. But removing has benefits, too. Verna Fields, the editor of *Jaws*, is widely credited with "saving" the movie by convincing director Steven Spielberg to cut early scenes of the mechanical shark. This removed several scenes with bad, distracting special effects. But it also significantly increased the build-up of suspense. The audience had to wait much longer to finally see the shark.

Ren & Stimpy was originally called "Your Gang" and *Calvin & Hobbes* originally had a bunch of other stuffed animal friends. In both cases, they were cut down from an ensemble to a classic double act.

Remember that status quo we need to be wary of? Well, the status quo in business is to 1) launch new products and 2) support existing product lines. There are many reasons to support existing products: you want to keep your retail partners happy, underperforming products may still bring in revenue, and employees' livelihoods are linked to those products. There is also the issue of sunk costs—the time, money, and effort getting those products launched. However, reversing course to cut out-of-date product lines or non-profitable products has a benefit: it frees up time, money, and effort to pursue more-promising projects.

After he recaptured his position as CEO of Apple, Steve Jobs cut 70 percent of the company's product line. There were too many unprofitable projects obstructing growth. The status quo bias made these cuts unpopular, but they were the right decision for the company. They made way for the creation of the iPod.

Google regularly asks, "What products can we kill?" The Google Graveyard has 194+ products, apps and services—and growing with the likes of Google+, Google Reader, Google Play, Google Hire, Google Trips, and of course, Google Glass.

BEWARE OF FEATURE CREEP

Sometimes it's not the product itself that needs to go, but specific aspects of the product.

Look at your remote control or microwave. How many of those dozens of buttons do you actually use? Software is notorious for this, too. Most designers and engineers (especially novice ones) think that experiences are based on an additive property. They keep adding features that actually get in the way of what you need for the product to function. The reason is that people choose products with more features, but they tend to only use a few of them—and the others get in the way.[36]

Sometimes removing what seems to be the most essential feature of a product is a good move. That is what behavioral economist Dan Ariely and his co-founders did with Shapa.

Do you pee *and* poop in order to lower your weight before you climb on your scale in the morning? As scales have become more precise with their digital readouts, every tenth of an ounce seems to matter (Wait. I ate four salads yesterday, and I gained .387th of a pound??).

---

36 Thompson, D. V., Hamilton, R.W. & Rust,R. (2005). Feature fatigue: When product capabilities become too much of a good thing, *Journal of Marketing Research*, 42, 431-442.

You may remember old scales where the needle never settled on one number. It just quivered in the general vicinity of a number. Well, the Shapa doesn't have a number. It doesn't have a readout at all. You still weigh yourself every day, and the Shapa sends your weight to a server. At the end of the week (or a month), you learn your average weight. The number is much more accurate than your standard scale because it gives you a more stable assessment. You can track your average over the month, six months, or a year. The benefit of no readout is that because of loss aversion, people are overly sensitive to when they are slightly heavier than they expect than slightly lighter than they expect. By presenting averages over time and away from the scale, you can get a steadier assessment of how you are doing—and can feel better about your progress.

The Shapa ends up giving more than it takes away.

DEVELOP YOUR SHTICK

Writing is hard. Writing is hard. Writing is hard.

This might be the most difficult chapter for you to implement in your life. I commend you for reading it.

Reading is like nutrition and writing is like exercise. Time to start exercising.

WAYS TO WRITE IT SO YOU DON'T REGRET IT

- If you want to get the gist of a topic, read a book about it. If you want to be proficient, read ten books about it. If you want to be an expert, write about it. Start reading and writing regularly. Put it on your calendar. Make it a priority.

- In writing, people err in two ways. They let the editor take too much control (often keeping them from creating at all, or at least never finishing), or they create and never edit. Which one are you? What are you so afraid of?

- Buy a journal. It's okay to spend some money on it—especially if it helps you write in it, so as not to waste money. On the other hand, if having a fancy journal makes it so sacred that it inhibits your writing, just get a cheapo spiral for 44 cents. Do what sets you free.

- Practice taking notes during a meeting. The meeting goes by faster, and you won't space out and start drooling, then get fired and replaced by a robot.

- Have a project idea? Start a one-pager. Someone pitching you an idea? Have them write a one-pager.

- Practice cutting your writing (use the 10 percent rule). When making other things, practice removing the non-essential from the things you're making. Removing the number of things to be made. Do less. And let what remains be better for it.

- Start tracking your writing. Note the days and times you do it. What gets measured, gets maximized.

The more you write—to remember, clarity, and communicate—the more you will take control of your ideas. You can architect your reversals, your steps, your chasms, your teams. You can intentionally sequence your actions to have the most impact. Because as you'll see in the next Act Out, the order of experiences matters.

ACT OUT: START STRONG. END STRONGER.

Comedian Phyllis Diller said, "Comedy is like a plane flight. The most important part is taking off and landing."

The landing part is obvious. Everyone knows how a good story has a great climax, and how a good joke has a punch line.

Stand-up comedians typically finish with their best material: the closer. It's the strongest material designed to get the most laughs. They open with their second strongest material: the hook. They hide their weakest material in the middle (which is the best time to go to the can during a comedy show).

I love the TV show *The Office* for countless reasons, but the cold opens are my favorite part of the show. You have seen the cold-open trend in film and TV—perhaps an action sequence that immediately hooks the audience—before the opening credits run. Sometimes they relate to the story, but they don't need to. When *The Office's* writers don't have to worry about moving the story forward, they can turn up the comedy and do something outrageous, such as where Michael hits Meredith with his car or Kevin drops his huge pot of chili in the office.

It's just an isolated bit, but it's hilarious. And then they hit you with the theme music.

Starting with strong material suggests that good quality material is going to follow. A lull after a strong start is okay because the audience knows what you're capable of and will be patient with you. I call this the *Promise Effect*.

Starting strong also helps you create an emotional reaction than leads to more emotional reactions. In the case of comedy, this emotion would be amusement, which helps make subsequent moments more amusing because you're already in a good mood. I call this the *Momentum Effect*.

If you don't have a captive audience—in other words they have an option to "escape," such as changing the channel or clicking to a different video, it is even more important to leverage the *Promise* and *Momentum Effects*. You can see that play in the creation of radio-friendly pop songs. They've got to hook you in seven seconds. In songwriting, the weakest verse is often the last.

Businesses create experiences for customers: events with a beginning, a middle, and an end. Most famously, Disneyland is a series of experiences, from the beginning of the ride to the end of the ride. Retail is also a series of experiences, from walking in the door to walking out the door. Customer service is an experience, from dialing to hanging up. A customer's experience must be positive in the moment, but maybe even more importantly, they must be positive in *hindsight*.

CHAPTER 6

WORK HARD OR HARDLY WORK

Imagine you are one of the world's most successful comedians—happily married, three kids, and worth nearly a billion dollars. You've just hit traditional retirement age. How do you spend your time?

Perhaps you buy a new home or two. You are prepared to send your kids to any college they want to attend, with a new car for each. You spend more time cooking and working out. And you ramp up your commencement speech schedule.

Or perhaps you do a sold-out thirty-five-show fall tour, tape a Netflix show that features your exotic car collection, write a book, and talk to anyone who is willing to listen about your joke-writing process.

You know who I am talking about.

Jerry Seinfeld's craftsperson-like approach to comedy has done more than turn him into one of the most successful comedians ever. It has also led him to a happy, successful, fulfilling life.

With the goal of helping you get better at what you do *and* enjoy your work and life more, I am going to teach you to be more like Jerry Seinfeld. Not the Seinfeld on stage, or the Seinfeld on TV, but the Seinfeld behind the scenes. The Seinfeld who's a blacksmith.

THE LIFE OF A BLACKSMITH

From the outside, the blacksmith's life looks like drudgery—sweating by the heat of the fire, swinging a heavy hammer, banging on metal all day long.

A blacksmith's mentality is the methodical, continuous pursuit of high-quality work. The best work. Each swing of the hammer is deliberate, shaping the raw metal precisely as the blacksmith intends. Each swing of the hammer matters. Each swing makes a dent. Each swing solves a problem.

It's not easy work, but it can be rewarding. After swing after swing, day after day, and week after week, the blacksmith has...a sword!

Imagine how epic it would feel to wield a sword in your hand, knowing that you made it. It's the same feeling a sketch comedian gets while watching a script get laughs on stage, or a runner finishing a marathon, or a product manager launching a product into the market.

But a blacksmith doesn't just work for the final product. Amidst the struggle and the sweat, there is a strange satisfaction. The satisfaction is not pleasurable—not like an afternoon snooze (or an afternoon delight). It's not about fun or excitement. However, while swinging the hammer, the blacksmith can be transported into what psychological scientists call a flow state.

You likely experienced flow at one point or another. It's a satisfying feeling where time seems to melt away. Where you get so absorbed with what you're doing, you lose track of what's around you. Sometimes your mind goes blank, but sometimes your mind is fully engaged with what you're doing. In sports, it's called being in the zone. Writers get it. Runners get it. Even product managers.[37]

Flow is best induced by fully engaging in a creative problem-solving task that puts you on the edge of your abilities. Flow comes when you let go of perfection, and

---

37 This might sound crazy, but when I was a graduate student I would have this experience analyzing a dataset. Three or four hours would go by, and I would forget to eat. Now, on a good day, this happens with my writing. Alas. It is not happening with this section. I just checked Twitter.

yet are still in pursuit of it. Rather than focusing on product, you focus on process. This dynamic tension between the two ignites your flow.

So while you are pursuing a sword—a single joke, a one-hour special, a one-pager, a pitch, a product launch, or a whole career—the act of pursuing it like a craftsperson produces something equally as amazing: engrossing, absorbing satisfaction along the way.

WILL IS OVERRATED

Let's get something straight: self-control is not the secret to becoming a successful blacksmith—or anything else, for that matter.

We like to romanticize those who achieve audacious goals by way of superhuman willpower. YouTube is teeming with motivational videos glorifying how "wanting it more than you want to breathe" will lead to success. We celebrate the great business successes that people achieve by force of will. We gobble up movies that show heroes who harness the eye of the tiger to attain greatness. It's a compelling narrative, great for training sequences in a *Rocky* movie. But it's largely fallacious.[38]

---

38 Even if you did want to spend months doing things like chasing a chicken around just to get ready for getting punched in the face, very few of us have access to a meat locker.

Sure, successful people do often have better-than-average willpower. Years of research reveal that an ability to delay gratification is associated with a wide array of professional and personal successes. But there are also years of research showing that people with the best willpower in the world are not always successful.

Further, leveraging willpower to achieve a goal is not sustainable. Taxing your willpower wears it out, uses it up. So even willpower that is working for you at any one moment will eventually fade, and you'll be stuck like every other schmuck.

What to do instead?

HABITS, NOT GOALS

Scott Adams is the creator of *Dilbert*, a serial entrepreneur, and an all-around smart, ornery guy. And you'd think that someone so successful is a big proponent of big goals. Not Adams. He eschews goals. "Don't have goals. Have systems."

Systems are behaviors that happen on a regular basis. Losing ten pounds is a goal. Exercising first thing in the morning is a system. Having a comedy special is a goal. Writing jokes by day and testing them by night is a system.

When you start looking behind the scenes at the world's funniest people, they have systems.

"Systems" is just a fancy way to say that the world's funniest people have more good habits than bad habits.

Wendy Wood, a psychology professor at USC, has done extensive research on how habits guide behavior, why they are difficult to create, and why they are also so hard to break. (Check out her book *Good Habits, Bad Habits*.)

To create good habits or break a bad habit, you often need to create a new context. Say you love milk chocolate, and you have a bowl of M&Ms on the counter at work. Your plan is to only have a few. But you walk by again and the bowl is still there, so you have a few more. You tell yourself, "Ok, that's all I'll have today." But then later on, sure enough, you grab a few more.

If the bowl exists, the temptation exists. If the temptation exists, willpower is in use. If willpower is in use, it is being depleted. And so you hold out as long as you can until your willpower gives out. Then you're filling your mouth with fistfuls of M&Ms—even the gross pretzel ones.

A much better way to create a new habit is to change your context. Move the M&Ms to a less-frequented part of the office. Put them in a jar that's a pain in the ass to open. Bury them in a bowl of better-for-you snacks, like nuts and raisins. Or ultimately, create an M&M-free world.

Habits rely on associations. Humans are associative machines. It's one of our superpowers. We are great at making connections between events—even bad connections. (Wearing your ratty old socks so your favorite team wins is an example.) One idea activates another idea. Tug one thread from an associative web and the signal bumps another thread. One event triggers another. Memory is built on associations.

Whether exercising daily or smoking two packs daily, the unconscious mind has learned associations that have become automatic. To build a habit you are essentially creating a new set of associations—weaving your mental web. "When X happens, I do Y." You will need some willpower at first, but if you routinize, the need for willpower fades.

So the first step to a better habit is a new context. The next thing you need is time. There isn't a magic number to how long it takes to create a habit. It doesn't take twenty-eight days per se, but the spirit of that idea is correct. At first it takes persistence and patience, but eventually the new behavior becomes automatic.

One of the best times to create new habits and break old habits is when you have a change in life: a new job, a new apartment, returning from vacation. This disruption of your normal routine frees you up to create new systems. New contexts can be created.

So stop whining about change and make some.

SHTICK FROM SHANE

I have my own spin on this idea of changing your associations. I love candy. I've had periods in my adult life where I was getting multiple stomachaches per week from eating too much candy. Do you know how embarrassing it is to be a nearly forty-year-old man-child on a Halloween diet?

I tried to quit candy many times but would relapse like a junkie. So I just started buying candy that I hate. Now if I want candy, I have to choose between black licorice, circus peanuts, or candy corn.

I can have candy any time I want. I just rarely want it.

THE BLACKSMITH METHOD

A comedian's brilliance is typically attributed to natural talent. No doubt, the masters do possess a naturally great sense of humor. But like any other endeavor—artistic, scientific, or entrepreneurial—talent is not enough. Becoming a master takes the effort and routine of a blacksmith. It requires creating a system to do the work, practicing meticulously, and then going and having some fun.

There are three critical elements to creating a craftsperson's lifestyle: protect, grind, and release. We are going to look at each in detail, so you can build your own blacksmith method.

PROTECT OR WRECK

The Pareto Principle is well-known in life-hacking circles. Applied to business, it states that 80 percent of your reward comes from 20 percent of your work. Of course, the actual percentages are arbitrary. The takeaway is that very little of your day-to-day work is what your boss or your customer really cares about.

If you don't know this (or choose to ignore it), then you end up prioritizing tasks that are pressing in the present but not rewarding in the long run. The common one is email. Email is urgent but it's rarely important. No one is ever going to look back on their career and say, "I was really successful because I was good at email." But email can easily hijack your workday.

SHTICK FROM SHANE

Much like a lot of jobs, 80 percent of my work is day-to-day BS that doesn't really move my long-term goals forward.

As a comedian and science podcaster, what people ultimately want are jokes and interesting insights. But 80 percent of my job is behind-the-scenes stuff. Driving from gig to gig, producing shows, being my own roadie, answer emails, booking guests, marketing, doing interviews.

Twenty percent is actually writing jokes and researching for shows and podcasts. Not only is it my favorite part, but it is the most important. As I continue to invest in myself, much of my money goes to paying to delegate as much of the 80 percent off of my plate. My product increases in quality, and I live a happier life.

As for my girlfriend who only gets to see me 20 percent of the time, I tell her that is the best 20 percent. She is 80 percent sure I'm lying.

So what is the small proportion of your work that brings in the most reward? How do you create an M&M-free world so you can regularly do your best, most-rewarding work?

It takes three steps. First, identify your most rewarding and productive creative work. Second, schedule time to do that work. And third, protect that time by any means necessary.

The third one is the toughest.

Looking to protect our creative time, most of us will pick up our laptop and go somewhere quiet that allows us to avoid distraction. Sure, you're sequestered in an office or a cafe, but you brought two distractions.

The first distraction is your damn phone.

A blacksmith doesn't need a cell phone. A blacksmith needs a forge and a hammer. Everybody knows that their phone is a distraction, but most don't seem willing to do anything about it. Get a handle on your phone by putting it down or leaving it behind. Use it for its usefulness and then let it go. Locking it up or turning it off ends up being critical for success.

Can you imagine if Alexander Graham Bell had had a distraction like a phone? He would have never had the focus to invent the phone.

Quentin Tarantino gets it. There are enough laugh-out-loud moments in Tarantino's movies that I consider him to be a comedy director (e.g., the Ku Klux Klan eyehole debate in *Django Unchained*). Making a movie is so difficult that Tarantino takes extreme measures to protect his on-set time. Tarantino wants everyone focused on being as productive as possible. He has a strict rule that there are no phones on the set. Use a phone and you are fired. Not even Brad Pitt gets to use his phone.

The second distraction is your Wi-Fi connection. Having your email browser open, web browser open, and access to the internet is the same as sitting in an open office space with a bunch of monkeys running around—without the joy of sitting in an open office space with a bunch of monkeys running around.

The blacksmith avoids Wi-Fi. Every day, the blacksmith does the same thing: build a fire, start the forge, lay out the tools. The blacksmith doesn't pause from swing the hammer to go to the village square to see what new notices are posted (or watch the latest public hanging).

HAVE YOU HEARD THE ONE ABOUT PROTECTING YOUR TIME?

It's easy to forget this, but *Seinfeld* was the biggest thing on television in the '90s. The show was incredibly funny, and it holds up well today. What made the show successful wasn't Seinfeld's acting chops. It wasn't the costumes or set design. Jerry Seinfeld and Larry David understood that 80 percent of the show's success was dependent on how funny the script was. And the script was only 20 percent of the work.

You can imagine their world. As lead writers (and for Seinfeld, the star) of a hit show, everybody wanted their attention. Approvals for this and opinions about that. The calls. The quick question that turns into a ten-minute conversation. Michael Richards busting through the door.

Their distractions were worse than anything you get in your inbox.

Seinfeld and David created a rule: when they were finalizing a script that they got from the writing staff, they would go into their office and close the door. As Seinfeld said, "The door was closed, it's closed. If somebody calls, we're not taking the call. We're going to make this thing funny." So while the door was closed, everything else was either on hold or the staff had to make their own decision.[39]

In order to ensure their best work, Seinfeld and David established a place and time that protected the most-important 20 percent of their work from every other aspect of life. Not just frivolous distractions, but *anything* that would interrupt their focused flow. This allowed them to be creative even without willpower.

---

39 The only person who had access when the door was closed was an administrative assistant who would type up rewrites. Every so often, Seinfeld or David would emerge to give her notes to type into a new script. Sometimes she would laugh out loud while typing up the script. They would bolt from the office to find out what line had her laughing.

JOB WITHIN A JOB

Protecting your time can come in many colors and, dare I say, shades of gray.

Claire Downs is a Los Angeles-based comedian, writer, and producer who is still hoping for her big break. Struggling to make ends meet, she has been taking temp jobs to pay her rent. This is not unusual. If you ever come to LA, there is a non-trivial chance that a comedian will workshop some jokes as he or she drives you from the airport.

Remember how comedians break rules to get ahead? Well, Downs doesn't let temping stop her from pursuing high-reward creative work. She has created a series of ethically ambiguous work hacks to make comedy on someone else's dime.

She tells people at work that she has a vitamin D deficiency, which is "not technically a lie" since most people are vitamin D deficient. This gives her license to take calls outside or work on the patio of a local café, away from the watchful eye of bosses and co-workers. She will also book a conference room for two hours for a "call," then close the door and write some comedy.

Her go-to hack is her "go bag," the backpack that she brings into the office. Well, the two backpacks that she brings into the office. Since many of the temp jobs provide her a computer, she stows her own laptop, books, and notes in a backpack and hides it inside another backpack. This larger backpack becomes the decoy.

Downs enters the office and sits at her desk like normal. Rather than procrastinate by scrolling through Instagram, she gets her temp work done as quickly as possible. When she's ready for her comedy work, she puts a coffee on her desk, strews candy wrappers around the work computer, and leaves the decoy backpack on the desk. She takes the *other* backpack to a quiet workspace elsewhere and works on her comedy.

As she told me, "You can go wherever you want because you look busy when you have all that crap all over. One time, I pitched a movie during the middle of the workday in Beverly Hills. My job thought that I was in the bathroom."

The takeaway: 1) don't hire Downs unless it is for a writer's room and 2) Downs has found a way to protect her craft with a bag within a bag, a job within a job. A grind within a grind.

GRIND IT OUT

A comedy special doesn't look like work. The comedian looks casual and relaxed (unless it is Sebastian Maniscalco running and jumping on stage). Their jokes land perfectly. They play the crowd like a virtuoso musician plays their instrument. Yet the making of a comedy special takes a tremendous amount of time and effort. It's usually the culmination of at least a year of hard work. Jerry Seinfeld has a method for creating a comedy special. It's called, "Don't break the chain."

When Seinfeld is working on a stand-up special, he gets one of those big, old-school paper calendars. He nails it to his wall in a prominent place. Every day that he works on his material, he makes a big X through that date. After three X's in a row, he has a chain.

Once the chain is in place, his goal becomes simple, even small: don't break the chain.

There's no avoiding the fact that you have to put in the work. But spacing the work out on a regular basis is superior to cramming. Working fourteen hours across seven days is much more productive than working fourteen hours in a day. Your ability to focus is better for those two-hour blocks and you end up wasting less time. Pulling all-nighters will not yield the same results as keeping the chain.

Start a chain and don't break it.

SHTICK FROM SHANE

When I started out in comedy, I worked temp construction jobs and would constantly sneak off to write jokes. Then I noticed that there were these security guys on the site that never seemed to do anything. So I asked them for a job. I got it. I am highly qualified at doing nothing. My job was to sit in one place and not fall asleep.

That was my time to develop material. I would always have a voice recorder going. Then I would go home and make my girlfriend listen to all my joke ideas and workshop them with me. (That relationship didn't last.)

I would record every one of my sets and figure out which words I could cut, so I could achieve more laughs per minute. I would rate the level of the laughs and get rid of the worst jokes from my act.

Because of this, I was the comic in town that always had more and better material than anybody.

That reminds me. I better start doing this stuff again, or I'll be forced back into temp work.

MASTERS OF THE GRIND

At seventy-five, Joan Rivers had the work ethic of a twenty-something founder of a start-up. Having open days on her calendar filled her with angst. To avoid it, she would crisscross the nation doing shows and events, taking red-eye flights in a way that would wear out the most energetic traveler. Her documentary, *Joan Rivers: A Piece of Work,* documents this.

Charles Schulz, the creator of *Peanuts*, drew every single one of his nearly 18,000 *Peanuts* comic strips by himself, without assistance, for over fifty years. He would write a daily strip and a Sunday page, week in and week out. This was clearly no easy task. How did he do it? Monday through Friday, five days a week, he would drive his kids to school. Then he would go to his studio and work on his strip until about 4:00, when the kids came home from school. That was his day. Between 8:30 and 4:00, day in and day out, he worked on the comic strip. Like Seinfeld, he would not break the chain.

In the early '70s, Richard Lewis started to get into stand-up comedy. He was living in New York City, doing open mics and small-venue shows wherever he could get them. Fellow comedian David Brenner saw Lewis's potential and lent him $1,000 so that Lewis could quit his day job and work exclusively in comedy. This is the equivalent of over $6,000 now. Richard made the most of it, performing 340 of 365 nights in a single year. Think Lewis got better at his craft?

A FARMER'S WORK ETHIC

Wil Anderson (the guy who forgoes set lists) is a grinder. He releases a new special every year, each one of them a play on his name: *Jagged Little Wil*, *License to Wil*, *Kill Wil*, etc.

Early in his career, Anderson would bring two suitcases on the road: one for clothes and the other for work. He would unpack his things, hang his clothes in the hotel closet, and put toiletries in the bathroom. Then he would set up his space for his daily comedy work, laying out notes, books, and newspaper articles on the hotel room desk.

Anderson comes from a family of dairy farmers, and he has a farmer's work ethic. He told me about his life as a youngster. Every morning, he got up early and milked the cows. There was no circumstance when that could be skipped. The cows must be milked daily. Period. "Must milk the cow" is Anderson's version of "Don't break the chain."

It's no surprise that he's one of the most successful comedians in Australia. And it only took him ten years to become an overnight success.

SHTICK FROM SHANE

When I moved to Boston, I found it easy to get jobs to pay the bills. I had this wholesome look, and people thought that folks from Wisconsin had that farmer's work ethic. Boy were they wrong.

The only thing I have ever worked hard for was my comedy. I have never called in sick for a gig.

My grind began at a weekly Wednesday night open mic in the worst bar in the worst part of the worst city in Massachusetts: the Emerald Isle in Dorchester, MA. There were two bathrooms but only one of them worked, and that was only for emergencies. The heating and AC never worked, so the room was always too hot or too cold—summers and winters in Massachusetts are a real joy. They never cleaned the tap lines, so ordering a draft beer was a mistake that no one made twice. Once while standing outside, I was mugged at gunpoint.

It was a true open mic: anyone who signed up would get the stage for five minutes. And anyone and everyone showed up. This meant that rather than the typical ninety minutes, the show ran over four hours. More is not better when it comes to comedy shows. Especially open mics.

There was never any actual audience, just comics waiting for their turn, chatting amongst each other and never paying any attention to anyone's set. It was a bit like crashing a party with a stand-up routine no one wanted to hear. To keep the comics around drinking all night, the bar owner would buy pizza toward the end of the night, and anyone who performed would get a slice. Because of this, homeless people would sign up for the open mic so they could be indoors and eat. WILL BOMB FOR FOOD.

The Emerald Isle was an experience most people tried once and you never saw them again.

I went to the Emerald Isle every week.

Each week I wrote a completely different five minutes to perform, which was unusual. I also took really big chances and tried to write stuff that would shock the unshockable degenerate comics who were my "audience." Because of this, sometimes I could get a couple comics to pay the tiniest bit of attention. I used to get one chuckle a week.

That's how I knew that I might just have a shot in this business.[40]

SWEET RELEASE

Most motivational YouTube videos will tell you to "Rise and grind." But if you pay attention to the books and articles on life hacking, you will see contradictory advice: boredom is beneficial. By letting yourself be bored you will generate ideas and insights that you never could if you were just grinding.

Both are right.

These ideas are not mutually exclusive. But most of us prefer one and forsake the other. Either you're not working regularly and hard enough—you don't protect and grind—or you're not taking some time away to allow yourself to regenerate. You need a break.

Jerry Seinfeld doesn't break the chain, and yet he finds time to take a break and meditate every day. He started back in the '70s. While making *Seinfeld*, everyone would go to lunch, and he would meditate for twenty minutes. He would often eat lunch after, while he was working. He attributes his meditation practice to how he survived the nine years of *Seinfeld*, which was seriously taxing work. Imagine the pressure of making the world's funniest show

---

40 Thank you, Ed Regal who ran the dump, and thank you Rich Gustus for hosting that train wreck. It was one of the best things that ever happened to me.

week in and week out. Jerry would find time away from his work in order to take care of himself.

To some business-minded readers, "meditation" might sound like a bunch of hippy talk typically reserved for goat yoga, animal horoscopes, and Gwyneth Paltrow products for your privates, but the science of meditation is very promising.

There is a long list of funny people who meditate that includes Howard Stern, Ellen DeGeneres, Russell Brand, John Mulaney, and Kristen Bell.

When you look at highly successful people, they have their daily habits working on their creative work. Then at some point, they release themselves from their work and go do other things. They all have activities where they can unwind and enjoy themselves.

One problem is that too many people don't create space between their grind and their release. They're trying to work all day long and simultaneously enjoy themselves all day long. But the world's most productive creative people have a distinct space between those two things.

Protect. Grind. Release.

A WALK IN THE PARK

"Want to know the secret to good comedy?"

Years ago, I was on a phone call with Alex Gregory, a cartoonist and comedy writer. I had recently started studying comedy, but I didn't have much knowledge or any real connections. I was feeling things out. He off-handedly says to me, "Do you want to know the secret to good comedy?" I'm like, "Um, yes please."

There was a brief pause, and then he said, "Long leisurely lunches." I was surprised. He continued with something like:

> When I'm working on a script with my writing partner, especially when we're kind of stuck on something, we go out to lunch, and we sit outside in a nice cafe. Sunny day. We just have a long, leisurely lunch, two-plus hours. We just talk about things until inevitably, the jokes start to flow.

It turns out that while plenty of comedy is about frustration and conflict and maddeningly annoying people, in the *making* of comedy, positivity and creativity go hand in hand. You have to compliment the grind by being a little lazy, taking a nap, going for a walk. All of those things are important. You must release.

Wil "the Grinder" Anderson recognizes that all releases are not the same:

> Sometimes when I'm writing, the best thing that I can do is sit down at the desk for hours working on a bit and then I'll go and clean the pool. I'll go and get some leaves out of the pool for twenty minutes and it will all fall into place because what you need to do is, now that your brain is working one way, if your body is half concentrating on something else, your brain starts working in a different way to when you're sitting down in front of your desk concentrating on the problem.

Black-out drunk is not a good release. Surfing the internet is not a good release. How's this for a good release? No electronics, bare feet, fresh air, sunlight, movement, people who energize you.

Good release looks distinctly different from your grind. A different context, a noticeable change. So get out of the fluorescent lights and away from the rectangular tables. Get out into nature. Spend time with friends and family. Spend time in the sun. Take a fifteen-minute walk.

SHTICK FROM SHANE

First off, never ask a comic how they release. OK, I'll restrain myself and give a serious answer.

I might have a slightly different take on this idea, and it seems to work for me. I never work that hard. I don't really carve out time each day for grinding out writing. I am always working. From most outside appearances, it doesn't look like I am working. A silly example is that, once in a while I might smoke some weed and watch *Animal Planet*. But that is work for me...in fact, I don't really care for weed. I only smoke it for work. I probably would have never had an interest in starting a science podcast had it not been for this.

But the single most important thing that I do is daydream... constantly. I love it. I've always been a daydreamer. It got me in a lot of trouble in school, but I found a way to make a living out of something that I do naturally.

What my teachers saw as ADHD, my audiences get to experience as creativity.

People close to me know that I am often in space. It's been maddening to most everyone I've ever had a relationship with. But to me, two minutes of daydreaming can lead to better ideas than two hours of trying to force myself to write when I'm not inspired.

When a thought occurs to me, I allow myself to "drift off." What might look like laziness or inattention from the outside are actually my most productive moments.

Pete might have told me I needed a joke in this section, but I wasn't paying attention.

GO TO EUROPE

During my podcast interview with Billy Merritt, our Pirate Robot Ninja taxonomist from chapter four, he talked about what it takes to become an elite improviser:

- Day one, take an improv class. (No surprise.)
- Day two, watch some improv shows.
- Day three, form a practice group to work on your improv.
- Day four, go to an indie jam. This is sort of a drop-in thing where a random group of people get together and do improv.
- Day five, stay away from the improv studio, and study comedy more broadly. Watch *Duck Soup*, *Fleabag, or Schitt's Creek,* read books about comedy and so on.
- Day six and seven, go to Europe.

Of course Merritt isn't suggesting you go to Europe literally. Rather, go to Europe metaphorically. That is, don't do any comedy; get away from it all and experience the world. Going to Europe means doing something exciting and fun that will spur new ideas. That might be going to a museum, going camping, going to the farmer's market, or going on a road trip.

This has a double benefit. One benefit is that it gives you a break from improv. Then you can look forward to going back to it. It's a reward for five days of hard work. The other is that it helps make you more interesting. Comedy is about the world. And getting out thrusts you into the world that you're supposed to be making fun of.

We all need this kind of perspective. Your grind will be a lot more productive after you've released.

IMPLICATION: CREATING A CREATIVE DAY

Excellence is not innate, and certainly not static. I was excellent yesterday. Today, not so much.

Excellence is the result of working hard in a deliberate manner to develop your natural talent. Anyone can start with some talent. The talent develops into real skill when they protect, grind, and release. These practices are how a master craftsperson makes their craft seem easy.

But today's working world is not often designed to make the most out of people's talents. Most companies have a less-than-ideal workspace layout and work schedule. So until your CEO reads this book and gets on board, it's up to you.

How do you take control of your time and space, and make it work for you? It's called job crafting.

Comedians don't like people telling them what to do,

which is largely why they don't work regular jobs. But the majority of us do have to work within organizational boundaries. We've got rules to follow. But even within this structured environment, there are many ways you can get what you need. People such as Claire Downs and her "go bag" have found a way to bend the rules, crafting a job within a job. Not that I'm encouraging people to do that per se, but the spirit is right.

It starts by figuring out what it is that you do. Not the pretty paragraphs HR tries to pass off as your job description, but your real job. What you *actually* do and get rewarded for. The 20 percent that has the most impact.

You'll find that there are two types of responsibilities that often come into conflict: creative tasks (producing something) and managing the creatives doing the tasks. Which are you? Or maybe you're a hybrid, in which case the question is—when are you each one? It's important to know, because they have different needs.

Creatives need to make unique stuff—designs, reports, computer code, product prototypes—so they need a large block of uninterrupted time. And ideally in an environment that helps them make the most of that time.

A manager's responsibility is to help the creatives be the best they can be. There is often conflict between managers and those they manage because some managers think they are more important and have "the power." But it's really the people who solve problems and, you know, *create* stuff, that add value (i.e., the creatives).

Manage doesn't mean control—it means helping to function at the highest level. Great managers look at their role as servant leadership. They see their job as supporting the creatives, not the other way around.

This doesn't always happen. Managers want to have meetings at their convenience. So they'll plop a meeting at 10 a.m. on a Thursday, right in the middle of the sweet spot for their creators. The figure below depicts a stylized version of research explaining how people's "tiredness" changes as the day goes on.[41]

41 Krueger, A. B., Kahneman, D., Schkade, D. Schwarz, N., & Stone. A. A. (2009). National Time Accounting: The Currency of Life. In *Measuring the Subjective Well-Being of Nations: National Accounts of Time Use and Well-Being*, ed. Alan B. Krueger, 9–86. Chicago: University of Chicago Press. Michaels, Guy. 2008.

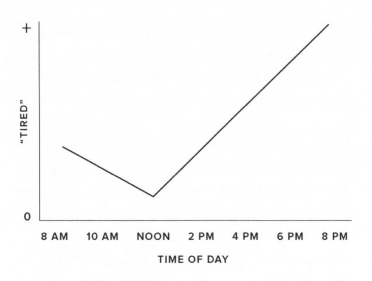

The majority of people have a lot of energy until about lunchtime. Then we naturally start to get tired. It's part of a natural cycle. Some cultures embrace this lull. (Siesta anyone?) But many don't. This means that most people are at their best in the morning when their day is getting started, making the morning the best time to be focused on the most important, creative tasks. But now, the manager's meeting has crashed the party, forcing the creator to break their flow in order to attend what is, let's be honest, usually a stupid meeting.

So for the managers out there: how can you protect your people's time and productivity? How can you help them grind at their best? And how can you release them to be their best day in and day out? Because the nature of creative work is so different than management, and frankly so strange, it requires a different kind of schedule. A creative schedule.

My thinking on this topic has been heavily influenced by Paul Graham. He is the co-founder of Y Combinator, arguably the most famous business accelerator and seed capital firm. By recognizing the need for programmers to be at their best creative selves, the managers bow down to the creative schedule and make managers' meetings secondary. In fact, they try to avoid meetings as much as possible. Managers keep office hours, a swath of time where they're available to talk and meet. Thus, the creatives can talk to the manager when it's best for them. And when they do need to have a traditional meeting, they're conscious to schedule it outside of prime creative time. This allows the creative to stay in *event time*, rather than being forced to follow *clock time*.

TAKE OFF YOUR WATCH

Research on people's perspective on time has identified that there are two very different types of people: clock-time people and event-time people.[42]

---

42 Avnet, T. & Sellier, A.L. (2011). Clock Time versus Event Time: Temporal Culture or Self-Regulation?, *Journal of Experimental Social Psychology*, (4) 665-667.

Clock-time people use time stamps to schedule their day. They block events out by the calendar and then fit the tasks to those times. They value being punctual. And they're not afraid to interrupt activities to move onto the next item on their schedule. Managers tend to be clock-timers.

Event-time people believe that things take as long as they need to take. They're much more flexible. They wake up when they wake up, and some days breakfast takes an hour. Or two. They let the situation and their feelings guide their choice of things that they do. Creatives are more likely to be event-timers.

This matters to a creative because when they are flowing they can keep flowing, rather than having to stop just because the clock says so. On the other hand, if they are stuck they can quit the task and do something else, rather than having to grind ineffectively until "time's up."

If you're already the CEO or a leader like Paul Graham, then it's currently in your power to restructure your team's work schedule and meeting habits to maximize creative time. If you're not the CEO, then it's your job to "job craft" as much as possible within the constraints of your organization. Block out productive time. Work remotely some mornings. Schedule fake meetings to block your calendar. Talk to your manager about having meetings later in the day. Introduce good behaviors to the team that can become habits.

SHTICK FROM SHANE

As you might guess, Pete is a clock-time person. I am an event-time person. We agree that we'd be a little better off if I was a little more clock time and he was a little more time event time. But mostly, Pete should become a little more event time.

Sometimes I go to bed at 9 p.m., sometimes I go to bed at 6 a.m. Sometimes I get off stage and I am exhausted and depressed and I want to go to bed. Other times, I get off stage and am energized and inspired and stay up writing all night. I don't force myself to work when I would rather go to bed and I don't force myself to sleep when I am inspired to work.

I try to be mindful of when I'm feeling my most inspired and productive, and milk it for all it's worth.

There are plenty of times I will do some light, relaxing writing to get myself inspired, but it just isn't the same quality if I force it too much.

So get off my back, McGraw.

DEVELOP YOUR SHTICK

Even if you embrace all the status quo-smashing mind-sets of the first five chapters, in order for it to amount to anything you've got to rock the creative trifecta: Protect + Grind + Release.

KNOW THYSELF

We all have our habits and our blind spots, so pay attention to yours. Get out of default and shift to intention.

- Quit trying to multi-task. Quit trying to use willpower. Quit social media. Minimize email. Do what it takes to create a distraction-free work time so you can do your essential work.
- Those of you who don't mind being distracted or *believe* you can multi-task: start protecting your productive time.
- Grinders (you know who you are): Stop burning yourself out. Protect your breaks and step away.
- Those of you who lounge too much (you know who are): stop waiting to begin. Protect your grind and get to work.

In all cases, intentionally show up fully present to whatever mode is called for in that moment—a master blacksmith knows when to pick up the hammer, and when to set it down.

CREATE YOUR RITUAL

I like to create rituals in my day. Habits and routines are boring, but rituals are special. Rituals are like a reward. The process itself becomes enjoyable. One of mine is that I treat myself to a delicious cappuccino (in a ceramic cup) before I write. When the cappuccino is finished, it's time to start.

- What rituals do you have?
- What rituals do you wish you had?

SHTICK FROM SHANE

When I get out of bed, the first thing I do is to breakdance for thirty minutes before I start my writing process.

Another thing I do is, when I don't feel like writing, I try to make up a lie to amuse myself. It gets me thinking absurdly.

STOP HAVING STUPID MEETINGS

One of the stupidest inventions is the sixty-minute meeting. Often a ten or fifteen-minute meeting will do. But meetings will always expand to fill the space you give them.

Managers: schedule meetings later in the day, rather than letting them take up prime creative time. And before you do, ask yourself:

- Does this really need to be a meeting?
- Could I schedule this meeting to minimize the effect on creative time?

- How long does it really need to be?

Creatives: grind in the morning and then release yourself in the afternoon. That's the time to go do other tasks, go have fun, take care of the email, etc. Intentionally focus on:

- How you protect your time and space from things like email and meetings and so on.
- Being comfortable not being available, saying no, delaying those minute tasks.

Because whether you're a creative or a manager, you're helping to make the thing that is ultimately rewarded: a book, a hit TV sitcom, a new piece of software.

In our next Act Out, you'll see that not only does it matter what time your meeting is, but where.

ACT OUT: TURN DOWN THE LIGHTS

If you've ever been to a good comedy club, you may have noticed that it's set up in a particular way: a dimly lit room, often in a basement with low ceilings. The familiar red brick background, a stool on stage, and a single mic on a stand. Oh yeah, and it's a little chilly.

These are purposeful choices. Comedy club owners engineer their space to maximize laughter. The behavioral sciences back these choices either theoretically or empirically.

DARKNESS

The room is dark because darkness helps create anonymity. The research on this is clear: people who are anonymous are more likely to behave without concern of what others think about them. This is important when you have a comedian onstage making risqué jokes. And most comedians do—because they're probing that line between benign and violation. With the lights down, no one can identify you as the person laughing at an off-color joke.

LOW CEILING

With high ceilings, the laughter of the audience rises in the air and evaporates. But low ceilings bounce the laughter back down to spread through the room. And the research on humor shows just how contagious laughter is. Hearing someone laugh can make you laugh without even knowing what they're laughing about. The effect of laughter as a contagious phenomenon is so powerful that in laughter yoga (yes, that is a thing), people start out fake laughing. Then it transitions into real, genuine laughter—what's called Duchenne laughter. That is true, joyful laughter.

COLD

The *Late Show* set was notoriously cold. Exactly fifty-five degrees. I know because I attempted to go one summer and received a written warning not to arrive in shorts and a T-shirt. I emailed Merrill Markoe to ask why Letterman wanted the set so cold. She responded simply, "DL liked it that way."

After some snooping, I found out that Letterman experimented with different temperatures. He found that the cold air made the audience more alert—something you want from a studio audience. The cold temps have an added benefit: he wouldn't sweat in a double-breasted suit under hot studio lights. So most good comedy clubs set the temperature low to keep the crowd alive and keep the comedian looking good.

CLEAN RED BACKGROUND

The red brick wall is part of tradition, an homage to the first comedy club in the United States, the Improv in Manhattan. Theoretically, red is helpful because it's more arousing than other colors. The research hasn't been done on red in comedy, but having a red background may enhance the audience experience, certainly more so than, say, having a blue background.

But, the red brick was an accident. Well, it wasn't intentional. Budd Friedman, the creator of the original Improv, wrote in his memoir that the Improv had previously been a Vietnamese restaurant with paneling-covered drywall. While renovating, Friedman tore down the paneling and drywall on the stage. Behind it was red brick. He left it because he was on such a tight budget he couldn't afford to do anything else.

Take the opposite of these things and it's no wonder that it's so tough to get laughs at church.

THE SUM IS GREATER

So all of these things make a great room. Sadly, there are

far more crappy club atmospheres than excellent ones. I interviewed comedian Todd Glass for my podcast. This man has thought more about comedy club design than any comedy club owner: just because the lighting goes up to ten on the board doesn't mean you put it up to ten... why paint a distracting mural on the wall behind the stage...and so on. He's now on a personal mission to fix bad comedy rooms.

As we talked about the value of different elements that make or break a club, I forced him to conduct a "Sophie's Choice" for what mattered most. His ordering was: 1. Cold, 2. Darkness, 3. Low Ceiling, and 4. Clean Background.

Immediately after giving this ranking, Glass countered that you really need all of these things. You can rank them but it's a lie. A surgeon wouldn't be able to operate in a room that has half the essential things that make an operating room great.

To promote *The Humor Code*, Joel and I did a survey of comedians to figure out the best comedy clubs in the nation. The winners had all four elements. In fact, in some people's eyes, some rooms were *too* good. At one point, the late-night talk shows began refusing to take any demo tapes that had been taped at the Ice House in Pasadena. The room is so good that it can make a mediocre comedian appear great.

One of those great clubs is Comedy Works in downtown Denver, which is owned by creator Wende Curtis. Comedians love Comedy Works. It's a favorite room of Dave Chappelle. Joe Rogan recently taped a special there. What's striking is that Curtis goes much further than red brick walls, low ceilings, cool temps, and dim lights. Don't like the bar food that Comedy Works serves? They will send someone down the street and get the comedian sushi. Most comedy clubs will rent a hotel room or have a flophouse-style apartment to house the traveling comedians. Not Curtis: she bought a one-million-dollar condo a few blocks from the club for comedians to stay in.

She's created a context that makes for happy comedians. This is quite the investment on Curtis's part, but now she has one of the best comedy clubs around, where world-class comedians love to perform. The comedians, the audience, and Curtis all win.

WHAT'S IN YOUR WORKSPACE?

The same consideration for context goes into designing the best places for people to work. As design firms like Gensler and OfficeUntitled know, a bad environment can stifle even the best talent.

Temperature and lighting are key elements in workspaces, just as they are in comedy clubs. Many of us have suffered through meetings in freezing or boiling conference rooms, and groaned under the pale and buzzing light of long fluorescent bulbs. But while anonymity is important for comedy, another factor for productivity is *privacy*.

You are probably aware that open-plan office spaces are all the rage. Cubicles and walls have been pulled out of offices around the world to make space for long, shared worktables. Dozens and even hundreds of workers may share the same open-plan space. This is all to encourage more interaction and collaboration among workers. More natural light is sometimes an added benefit. Also, they look much cooler than cubicles.

As it turns out, open-plan offices are mostly a bust. They're generally loud and distracting. Most people resort to noise-canceling headphones just to do work. And recent research shows that both worker interaction and productivity usually go *down* when people or offices move to open plan.

But critically, open offices provide no *privacy* for sensitive conversations or calls. The best workplaces have the option for open and closed environments where people can quickly and easily transition based on needs. Cloth-sided cubicles might be ugly, and personal offices might create pissing wars for the best space, but they provide both visual breaks and noise dampening. This gives people *some* privacy—which, it turns out, is important for being productive.

You don't have to be a major multinational company to design a workspace right.

Charlie Merrill is a physical therapist in Boulder who created a space to optimize results. He invented the Merrill Method, a cutting-edge approach to addressing pain. The method requires an in-depth intake interview with his clients, where he spends an hour asking questions and listening before he ever touches the person or has them move. In order to facilitate this intake, he got rid of everything in his office that made it feel like a hospital. Most important to the space are two very hip-looking comfy chairs that he brought in. He begins each session sitting eye-to-eye with his patients while they talk and he takes notes. And then when it's time, they move to an open area or his treatment table to start the physical diagnosis.

Think about how different this is from the typical experience in a medical setting—with you sitting awkwardly at an examination table while a doctor awkwardly stands over you trying to get through the conversation as quickly as possible.

Don't be afraid to step out of the stream to create the

atmosphere that supports what you need to cooperate to innovate.

CHAPTER 7

TAKE A BIGGER STAGE

How do you get Bill Murray to be in your movie?

You can't call his agent. He doesn't have one. You have to find someone who knows his 1-800 number. That's right. His 1-800 number. He's still doing movies, so you know somebody has it. So you have to figure out who has it and then convince that person to give *you* the number. That's not easy, because no one wants to be the dumbass who gave some other dumbass Murray's number.

Suppose you are good and lucky and get the number.

Then you call the number. "Hi, I am a producer, director, and writer. I have an exciting new movie project...blah, blah, blah."

You hang up. You wait and hope. And if you are good and if you are lucky, you get a call out of the blue. The person on the other line will say, "Mr. Murray's interested in your project. Please send a one-page write-up of the project to this PO Box."

You feverishly write up your one-pager and put it in the mail.[43] You wait and hope. And if you are good and if you are lucky, you will get a call. The person on the other end of the line will ask you if you can meet Mr. Murray on Thursday.

In Dublin.

"No? Okay. What about Saturday at 3 p.m. at LAX?"

Yes! You arrive at LAX at 3 p.m. There is a black car waiting for you—with Bill Murray in it. Bill Freakin' Murray!

After a long drive, you arrive at a house where you two will have dinner and discuss the project. And if you are good and if you are lucky, at the end of the meal, Mr. Murray will say, "Let's make a movie."[44]

Famous people are wealthy but rarely free. Murray has

---

43 If you have listened to me, you already have a one-pager.

44 The only person exempt from this is Wes Anderson, who has directed Murray more than anyone else. When Wes calls, he immediately says yes.

found ways to maximize his freedom. He has a 1-800 number and a PO Box. He buys one-way tickets when he flies so that he can decide when to come home based upon how much fun he's having. (That's an event-time person for you.)

And he has a good time. Crashing bachelor parties, riding a child's bike through Walmart, photobombing engagement photos, convincing Starbucks baristas to put some whiskey in his eggnog, doing karaoke with strangers. And my favorite: he walks up to people on the street from behind, covers their eyes with his hands, and says, "Guess who." When they turn around and see him, he says, "No one will ever believe you," and just walks away.

Legendary.

STAGED FOR SUCCESS

When you're looking to build a serious career, you've got to think growth. And to do to that, the masters of comedy move beyond their status quo—even when it's working. They've got to be willing to leave this stage behind and move on to the next one, the bigger one.

And so do you.

For you to find your own version of a legendary life, think

bigger. We'll look at three ways: going to a bigger place, finding a bigger platform, and taking a bigger perspective.

First up: it's not go big or go home. To go big, you may have to leave home.

A BIGGER PLACE

For many, taking a bigger stage means that they go to a bigger place. Literally.

To find opportunities to grow, Trevor Noah packed a suitcase and moved from Johannesburg, South Africa to the United States. Rebel Wilson moved from Sydney, Australia to Hollywood. Jim Jefferies went from Perth to Sydney to London as his star grew, and then to the United States.

If you are old enough, you know Yakov Smirnoff's jokes:

> In Russia we only had two TV channels. Channel One was propaganda. Channel Two consisted of a KGB officer telling you, "Turn back at once to Channel One."

He was working cruise ships in the Black Sea (he called them the Love Barges). In 1977, after two years of trying, he finally made it to the USA. But since he couldn't speak English, Smirnoff needed a translator. When the immigration official asked him his profession, Smirnoff said "comedian." Unfortunately, his translator picked "party organizer" as the translation. Smirnoff was nearly sent back to the Soviet Union the next day.

Often, aspiring young comedians move to the Big City to try and get their break. Sometimes this happens after a big break.

Gad Elmaleh is the Jerry Seinfeld of France. He's a superstar, mobbed everywhere he goes by fans clawing for autographs. He decided he wanted to take on a bigger place, and—as I'll address shortly—a bigger platform. So he moved to the States. As a smart comedian, he made a Netflix show called *American Dream* that spoofs his "fish out of water" journey. The show opens at his arrival at LAX. He approaches the passport agent and asks for the VIP line. The agent waves him over to the line with everyone else.

Elmaleh jokes about his move in his Netflix stand-up special:

> I've been doing stand-up in France for twenty-three years, and I just moved here and am starting over.

> I'm sure you've heard this story many times, about the man who moved to America with $1.00 in his pocket. And he worked so hard, and he made a fortune.

I moved here with a fortune.

Same story, guys, but I just did it backward. Which is harder, by the way. Because if I want to keep the same lifestyle that I had in Paris, and I don't make it here in America, I am going to go back to Paris with $1.00 in my pocket.

MAKING YOUR MOVE

In the world of comedy, New York is seen as the place to develop and Los Angeles is the place to cash in.

I talked about these ideas with Joe Rogan on his podcast. I put forth the hypothesis that a comedian should seek to be the biggest name in their city, in the same way that every major city in the United States has a local rap star (e.g., Pittsburgh has Wiz Khalifa, Houston has Scarface). At some point a local rap star becomes a big star and moves to LA or New York.

So my thought was that when you're the comedy equivalent of Wiz Khalifa for your city, you move. But Rogan saw it differently. To him, the sooner a comedian can make the move, the better:

> You need to be around other comics that kick ass. It's super important. It's important every step of the way. You need to be around them hanging out. You need to be around

them going onstage. We feed off of each other. We feed off of each other in a way that I don't think rappers—I mean I might be wrong, but I don't think they have to as much because they can kind of judge themselves on the long history of rap nationwide.

To Rogan, a comedian should get a general proficiency—thirty minutes of good material—and then, "Get the f*ck out of there. Gotta go to LA or New York."

But going to a bigger place is not just about getting reps. It's about connections with the people who will inspire you. He went on:

> Because you got to be around beasts. You got to see Bill Burr drop in to the Comedy Store on a Tuesday night and do fifteen minutes. You got to see Joey Diaz go up in the Original Room at 11 o'clock and murder the place. You got to see those guys. You got to be around them. There's a certain inspirational heat that you get from being around a crew of comedians that takes your act to the next level. Almost universally.

Tiffany Haddish is one of today's top comedians, but her first role as a paid performer was at El Camino Real High School in Woodland Hills, LA. She wanted to be a cheerleader, but the structure, the rules, and the rigidness of the squad turned her off. Instead she became the school's mascot: a Spanish Conquistador. She could basically do whatever she wanted and took to riling up the crowds not just with her physical antics, but on the microphone— something that no other mascot in the district did. She was so good that the school began paying to keep her as the mascot.

What helped her get her start, however, was being in the right place. As a fifteen-year-old, she was sent to comedy camp at the Laugh Factory on the Sunset Strip. While there, she got a stern lesson from...Richard Pryor...to "have fun." Because if you have fun as a performer, that will make it fun for the audience. Clearly this is something she did as a Conquistador.

And you never know who you'll meet or what it will lead to.

COOPERATING THE MOVE

For many years, the top comedians in Denver were a comedy trio called The Grawlix. Ben Roy, Adam Cayton-Holland, and Andrew Orvedahl had a monthly stand-up and sketch show. Then they wrote a spec script for a comedy show and submitted it to an Amazon Prime competition. They made the top ten but didn't win. However, they were able to sell the show to TruTV, and they went to Los Angeles to make it.[45]

When the Grawlix left Denver, that made room at the top for the next tier of comedians to step up and fill that void. But it didn't happen. Six or seven Denver comedians all made the move to LA at the same time. That seems peculiar, given the opportunity that had just opened up in Denver. But when "Cooperate to Innovate" informs your thinking, it makes more sense.

Luisa Diez—a New York City comedy booker and anthropologist—talked about this with me on my podcast:

> In the last several years, these other scenes built up that had some rank and some good talent there like Denver, Chicago, and New Orleans, for a minute, Atlanta. They built up enough talent and had enough platforms where their talents developed skills and got good enough to move to New York and LA. But instead of moving by themselves, they started moving in groups. Denver moved in groups. Chicago moved in a group. New Orleans was probably one of the earliest ones I noticed.
>
> What this did is they created this safe little nest for them-

---

45 The show is called *Those Who Can't,* and it's about high school teachers who are more immature than their students. I'm just glad they didn't make the show about university professors.

selves, because if six of you who already knew each other for a few years and watched each other come up moved to the city at around the same time, you all start shows, then you all book each other on your shows. Now you can trade spots with other people and your network becomes stronger than having to be around a couple of years until people recognize your face.

Again, it's not just about cashing in. It's about developing.

YOUR SECOND CHOICE

Richard Florida is a demographer at the University of Toronto. His most recent book is called *Who's Your City?* It's a terrible name for a book, but it has a fascinating premise. He argues that where you live is likely the second most important decision you make in your life (after who you marry, assuming you do). Because where you decide to live is going to dictate many of the opportunities that you have—in terms of the potential jobs, the quality of those jobs, the quality of people you'll work with, and thus the amount you can learn and the wealth you can build. (Also whether you have access to a good Philly cheesesteak, Chicago style pizza, or Wisconsin cheese curds.)

For a certain class of jobs, there's only a handful of places that you can go to be really successful in that field. For example, if you want to get into fashion, you want to go to New York or Paris or Milan. Your upside can be limited by the place you begin, so making that move to a bigger place can be necessary to take your career to the next level. Big cities tend to be the place.

Half the U.S. population lives in metropolitan areas. These urban centers are going to continue to grow. It's a hard decision to move a company's headquarters, but companies will move to bigger cities when they need better talent, more opportunities to collaborate, more customers, and more capital. These were the reasons Chipotle cited when it moved its HQ from Denver to LA. In 2018, General Electric moved from Fairfield, CT, to Boston. Dyson will be moving from Malmesbury (about two hours east of London) to Singapore in order to be close to its manufacturing and a rapidly-expanding Asian market.

Dorothy may think there is no place like home, but sometimes to find your full potential you need kick Wyoming to the curb. Sorry, Wyoming. Yellowstone is still amazing.

SHTICK FROM SHANE

I took a bigger stage by moving to Boston, but I actively avoided New York and Los Angeles. There can be an advantage to being out of the spotlight. In fact it can give you an edge. Being unknown gives people the feeling that they found a hidden gem. Agents, managers, and late-night bookers want to be the one who discovered someone and gave them their break.

In 2007 I was selected for the HBO US Comedy Arts Festival. It was the biggest festival in the country and one of the better opportunities for a young comic. I was the last of twenty-four new comics picked. Most comics already had some buzz in the industry and would later go on to do much bigger things than I ever will. People like John Mulaney, Kyle Kinane, and TJ Miller had everyone excited before the festival even started. The thing is, this festival was about discovering someone, yet a ton of these comics were already in NYC and LA. That meant the industry had already seen them doing their best material many times.

When I took the stage, no one had ever seen me, and I took everyone by surprise. I ended up winning the award for Best Stand-Up at the festival, getting myself a manager, an agent, and a spot on late night TV.

A BIGGER PLATFORM

Another way of finding a bigger stage is not necessarily a bigger place. It's a bigger platform—your reach.

In the late 1970s, Steve Martin became the biggest stand-up on the planet by leaning into a self-imposed constraint: he would not let himself tell the garden variety set-up and punchline jokes that were so popular on the late night TV circuit. Instead he juggled, made balloon animals, and acted like a wild and crazy guy. In my favorite bit, he would take the entire audience out of the club and onto the street. Just because. At his peak, he was selling out arenas. The crowds were so big, he started wearing a white suit so that everyone could see him on stage. He also appeared on *Saturday Night Live*, starred in movies, wrote movies, and directed movies.[46]

When you look at someone's career, you see a snapshot. You see their curriculum vitae. But if you look closer, you see that all those amazing things unfolded and built up over time. Martin didn't start out world-class. He pursued skill in one area and then leveraged that to move into a new area, all the while gaining a wider reach.

A blacksmith that went from building swords to building skyscrapers.

PLACE TO PLATFORM

Taking a bigger platform is a distribution play. You can

---

46 Martin recently won a Grammy for his banjo playing. Yes, a Grammy. He started playing when he was nineteen years old. Though he wasn't very good, he reasoned that if he practiced the banjo every single day, "in forty years I'll be really good at the banjo." Well, it took him more like 50 years; in any case Martin knows how to grind.

make this happen by leveraging your success in one area to reach more people in another.

The Marx brothers started out in Vaudeville before Broadway (a bigger stage) and then to the cinema (i.e., the biggest stage of their day). Even in the world of comedy, people break out and move beyond comedy. Ellen DeGeneres became a rival to Oprah in the daytime talk show space. Jamie Foxx went from stand-up to hip hop albums to Oscar-worthy performances.

It's not surprising we find specific places that become hotbeds for talent. The Improv in New York. The Comedy Store in LA. Second City in Chicago. These places are simultaneously cooperative and competitive.

Whether it be the set of *Saturday Night Live* or an improv house teams, the success of those people and those places begets success for more people in those places. And then the industry starts to look to those places for talent. Upright Citizens Brigade became a feeder for sitcoms in the same way that The Comedy Store became a feeder for HBO specials. Second City became a feeder for *Saturday Night Live*, and then *Saturday Night Live* became a feeder for movies.

These bigger places often lead to bigger platforms.

And if you're feeling stuck miles from where you want

to be, whether it's place or platform—have no fear. All it takes is personal intention to shift gears. Maybe to reach your ultimate goal you'll need to start out in a different industry. You can chart your course, picking up new skills as you traverse your way through the long game.

And you may find that the experience you've had off the beaten track is your differentiator that gives you an edge. Nothing is wasted when you know how to leverage it.

LEVERAGING YOUR EQUITY

Just like all the avenues to a bigger stage, shifting to a bigger platform often occurs in phases.

Say you're Coca-Cola. When you first start out, your focus is on growing your name recognition, teaching people what you offer, and showing them how it will bring them happiness. You begin very narrow and get known for one thing: cola in a curvy glass bottle. The more your brand becomes known for—and positively associated with— your niche, the more brand equity you create.

Once you have positive brand equity, you can leverage it to expand the platform. Often the first place to expand is within the established product line, aka *product line extensions*. So Coke begets Diet Coke and Cherry Coke. This also includes new packaging extensions—cans, plastic bottles, 2-liter bottles, fountains, etc. These increase the chances that people will buy your product, but often impact your brand equity in subtle ways.

Later you can leverage your equity to shift to something new; these are known as *brand extensions.* One of the most successfully flexible brands has been Richard Branson's Virgin. His first venture was a magazine he put out when he was seventeen years old. The Virgin brand launched in 1970 when he started selling mail-order music. A music store shortly followed. Seven years later it was a music label that signed the Sex Pistols. In the 1980s, Virgin got into things like travel, hospitality, and videogames. By the 1990s, Virgin's brand extension frenzy was in full swing, with Branson trying everything, seemingly with abandon: an airline, apparel, bridal, cinema, cosmetics, radio, television, and more. Many of these ventures were short-lived. Today Virgin still has over sixty active ventures, one of which is venture capital.

These brand extensions sometimes go *too far.* Dr Pepper knew that people were using their soda in barbecue recipes, so they decided to launch their own sauces & marinades. Bic went from making disposable pens to disposable razors to...disposable pantyhose. And Colgate decided they could leverage their brand equity into a growing market: frozen dinners.

MAKING THE SHIFT

When you're looking to expand your platform and influence to gain more control over your career, you need to think about your career in new terms: who you work for, and in what industries.

Platform is more than the city you live and work in. Platform is the kind of reach you want. Your goal may not be that of a typical comedian—to make a couple hundred people laugh in a theater. Perhaps you'd rather make millions laugh at the movies (or insert your industry equivalent). When you do this, you can spot opportunities with bigger reach and bigger resources.

But what is the bigger platform that allows you to capitalize on your abilities? And when should you take the risk to go for that new opportunity? These are important questions that we often avoid thinking about, mostly because they might prompt us to change.

You're stepping out of the stream, creating chasms, cooperating to innovate, working hard or hardly working so that you can have the career you've always dreamed of. One that creates viral, incredible things.

So when you're looking for your bigger and better platform, it's important to consider that your best opportunity may await you in a different company, a different industry, or a different medium.

A BIGGER PERSPECTIVE

Comedians ask "why" when writing jokes, but they ask "why not" when living their lives. Inspired by that observation, here's a final personal story.

As a professor, I go to academic conferences. In order to make the trips less boring, I host a dinner, typically on the last night of the conference. I invite a group of professional (i.e., business) friends who have become personal friends.

This dinner is filled with impressive people who are professors at elite business schools. Most of these folks got their PhDs from elite private universities. They are accomplished researchers and teachers, and some, I suspect, will go on to become deans or university presidents.

I limit the seating to eight people because you can't get any larger than that and maintain one group conversation. There are regulars and there are backups if the regulars aren't available. I'm a tyrant. To make the dinner run smoothly, I have rules: you can't invite other people, you've got to show up on time, etc. The regulars make fun of me for this and have affectionately dubbed this event The McGraw Dinner. The group enjoys kvetching about my rules, but they appreciate that we don't have any loose cannons who hijack the dinner to talk about their research methods.

I do a lot of talking. I can't help myself. However, during a dinner many years ago, I decided to be quiet and listen. I listened to the way the table talked about their professional challenges. And if you are a professor at one of these top schools, there are a lot of challenges. Acceptance rates at the academic journals are below 10 percent. Students are demanding. The workload is withering. There is a saying in academia about how flexible the job is: you can work whatever eighty hours you want.

I noticed something striking about how the group talked about professional challenges. The group spoke of these things like they were temporary irritants in the way of the great things they were doing. These challenges were not lions or snakes. They were mosquitos to be squashed.

PROMOTE OR PREVENT

The McGraw Dinner group has what psychologists call a promotion focus. A promotion-focused person is focused on achieving success.[47]

---

47   Higgins, E.T. (2005). Value from regulatory fit, *Current Directions in Psychological Science*. 14, 209-213.

I grew up prevention-focused. I grew up in a family with a single mom who didn't go to college. No one in my family ever earned a graduate degree. It wasn't terrible. We were food stamps poor, but not welfare poor. I was a public school kid. I went to state universities.

In a prevention-focused world, you want to avoid failure. You don't want a big house; you want to keep your tiny townhouse. You don't want fame and success; you want to hold on to your modest job.

Both promotion- and prevention-focused people can be successful in life, but what motivates them is very different. A promotion-focused person studies hard to get an A on an exam; a prevention-focused person studies hard to not get an F. They might both do well on the exam, but the way they feel about the exam is completely different. Promotion-focused people and prevention-focused people can both have a successful career, but the way they feel about their career and about executing tasks is completely different.

Here I was sitting at a dinner table filled with promotion-focused people, and I started to feel like an outsider—and I was hosting the damn thing.

Then I remember thinking, "Why not me?"

A life-changing moment in time. Yes, they went to better schools. Sure, they were working at elite universities, and I was at a state school. Fine. But I'm still sitting with them. They see me as a peer. Now, in order to be successful, I might have to be a little bit more creative, I might have to spend a few more hours in the laboratory on a Saturday night, but so far I've been able to do it. Why can't I learn to think bigger? Why not me?

Ever since that moment, I've worked hard to build my awareness about the way I'm thinking. If I catch myself trying to avoid failure, I focus on achieving success.

The lessons in this book are designed for promotion-focused people. Can you be one of them?

SHTICK FROM SHANE

Pete's story reminds me of how comics often measure success in the wrong ways when they first start in the business. Young comics ask me, "How do I get an agent?" Your agent usually shows up too late. You get a deal and then your agent is suddenly available. My big breakthrough has been getting a full-time assistant. Instead, I think they should be asking, "How can I get ahead without an agent?"

Sure, without an agent representing you, you might end up putting time into a book that you aren't getting paid for, but at least you will be in a book read by *dozens* of people.

Looks like Shane is just a step away from his own 1-800 number.

IMPLICATION: RADICAL SABBATICAL

Every seven years, I get a year sabbatical at half pay to move somewhere new, read more, write new things, and develop new ideas. No teaching load. No administrative work. It's a gift. This book is happening in large part because of one such sabbatical. Joe Rogan will finally be proud of me for coming to LA to write and get connected to the comedy community.

The average person, especially the average American, gets a couple weeks of vacation a year, and they're certainly not offered a sabbatical by their employer.

Being on sabbatical does not mean you sleep 'til noon every day. It means that you step away from the regular grind to find a new day-to-day. Invest in something that you can't maintain with your typical grind. Take this time to do whatever it is you've been putting off. Maybe it's decompressing or maybe it's digging even deeper.

I regularly encourage my business friends to consider a sabbatical. Take three, six, nine months away from a job. Read more books and travel to different places and expose yourself to ideas. Maybe make something that you couldn't have within your normal schedule.

Almost invariably, my business friends say, "I can't imagine doing that."

I say get a better imagination. Sure, you may not be able to do it right now. But if you set it as something that you want to be able to do, you could do it.

First step: Have enough money saved to be able to live on it. Cut your burn rate.

Second step: ask your boss for a sabbatical. You sit down with your boss and say, "I'd like to take a six-month sabbatical. I want to work on X, Y, and Z things that will make me a better salesperson/programmer/copywriter/supply chain guru." And you wait and you hope. Your boss is going to say no. Of course. Your boss doesn't want to lose you for six months.

So the next day you come in and hand your boss a letter of resignation. Your boss is not going to say, "Sorry to see you go." Your boss is going to say, "Let's talk about that sabbatical."

I was kidding. Asking your boss is the third step. The second step is to follow the Work Hard or Hardly Work advice and ensure you are your division's best salesperson/programmer/copywriter/supply chain guru. Be good enough at what you do that if you need to quit your job to make it happen you can find another one.

If you do that, the fourth step is to come in and hand your boss a letter of resignation. Your boss is not going to say, "Sorry to see you go." Your boss is going to say, "Let's talk about that sabbatical."

The small perspective is, "I'm just going to work this job for thirty years and then I'm going to live a remarkable life when I'm retired."

Take a bigger perspective. Ask "Why not?" Maybe that sounds privileged and ridiculous. But if you're here reading this book, you are smarter than average. You're willing to think beyond the obvious to find solutions that are transformative. Figuring out how to take a sabbatical is just a creative problem to be solved. You're not a robot.

Do some planning, run the numbers, cut back on your spending, and develop those skills.

DEVELOP YOUR SHTICK

To reach your full potential, you may need to make some changes. Even if you feel you are on the path to your chosen definition of success, don't be afraid to consider what exists outside the lines.

REEVALUATE YOUR TARGET

Ask others what you need to stop doing or what risks they think you should take.

Think bigger. Create a BHAG—Big Hairy Audacious Goal.

REVALUATE YOUR PATH

Hone in on your platform goal—and the path to get there— by asking yourself:

- What kinds of businesses are thinking big versus small?
- What would be that bigger platform to capitalize on your abilities?
- When do you put yourself in that position?

By working with bigger brands that have better resources, you are more likely to get better opportunities that expand your own reach and influence.

Ask yourself: is it possible for me to reach my definition of success in the company or industry I am currently in? Does it provide me with the platform I need to reach my goals? If the answer is yes, then stay the course. Protect, grind, release.

If the answer is no, then consider what you gain by remaining in the platform you're in and what you lose. Consider the ideal circumstances to seek a bigger platform. This may mean leaving your current job for a bigger organization, or even leaving to strike out on your own.

For our final Act Out, we'll look at what is arguably the most difficult way to grow: just say no.

ACT OUT: GETTING
FROM YES TO NO

A comedian trying to build a career has an outbound mindset. Hold a spear and hunt for opportunities. You're saying yes to lots and lots of things. To everything! Want to meet for coffee? Yes. Want to be on this podcast? Yes. Want to write this spec script? Yes. Want to be on my stand-up show? Yes. Want to donate a kidney? Yes. Wait. What?

Saying yes is useful—providing exposure and opportunity to develop comedic chops. An outbound mindset absolutely helps facilitate success. But at some point it also limits you.

Imagine you are a comedian, such as Hannah Gadsby, Hannibal Buress, or even Shane Mauss. Someone who has had some career success. You might just keep doing the same thing that got you to where you are. After all, you worked so hard to create a context for positive habits that help you level up your game. Why would you change it? After you've figured out *to do X in order to achieve Y*, it's easy to get locked into it. Rinse and repeat. But no one tells you when it's time to change the Y.

But so many don't shift. They stay in that outbound mindset and keep throwing spears at every opportunity that comes along. The more successful you get, the more you have to do. Success comes with its own administrative load, staff to manage, work obligations, and additional opportunities. And that stuff can get in the way of what you *really want* to do.

Smart, successful folks start to defend against the inbound offers—they pick up a shield. They say *no* to the things that are not the work they most want to do. They crowd out the small stuff. Stop hunting the small game and seek much, much bigger things.

Not everyone can have a 1-800 number as a shield. You must learn to say "no."

For the most part, we've been rewarded our whole lives for saying yes. Growing up, our parents teach us to say yes to them instead of no. Early in your career, saying yes is the way forward. People like you when you say yes. You're disappointing when you say no.

This seems especially challenging for women in the workplace. Research reveals that women often take on extra duties because the men in the office are saying no and the women in the office have difficulty saying no.[48] This ends

48 Babcock, L., Recalde, M.P., Vesterlund, L., & Weingart, L. (2017). Gender differences in accepting and receiving requests for tasks with low promotability. *American Economic Review*, 107, 714-747.

up harming them more than helping because these are often the kinds of duties that are not rewarded and do not lead to promotion. The importance of learning when to say no and then actually saying no is crucial. However, research also reveals that when women say no they are viewed less favorably than when men do.[49] This catch-22 means that women are damned if they do and damned if they don't. Sadly, there are no obvious solutions to this, except to figure out your individual approach to the trade-off.

Presuming that you're not a sociopath, saying no is difficult because no one likes disappointing other people. So people tend to apologize when they say no. "I'm really sorry. I can't do it. I'm just way too busy these days." Does that sound familiar?

The worst choice would be to say yes to something that's not moving you toward your goals. The second worst is to say, "I am sorry, but I can't because I'm too busy."

Apologizing for saying "no" makes you look bad. By saying "I'm sorry," you're suggesting that you're doing something wrong. You're not. Moreover, when you attri-

---

49 Keck, S. & Babcock, L. (2017). Who gets the benefit of the doubt: The impact of causal reasoning depths on how violations of gender stereotypes are evaluated, *Journal of Organizational Behavior,* 3, 276-291.

Heilman, M. E., & Chen, J. J. (2005). Same behavior, different consequences: reactions to men's and women's altruistic citizenship behavior, *Journal of Applied Psychology*, 90, 431-441.

bute it to being busy, you're suggesting that you don't have control over your life. And so you're inviting that other person to view you as reactive or undisciplined.

Here's a shield: "Thank you for thinking of me. I am flattered. Unfortunately, however, I am unable to do it."

Full stop. End of discussion. Shut your pie hole.

By thanking the person, you are acknowledging that they see the request as a positive opportunity. By saying "unfortunately," you're acknowledging your response may be disappointing. By saying you are unable to do it, you don't leave much room for negotiating. Because you are not negotiating.

SHTICK FROM SHANE

This advice is going to be useful for me. I crisscross the country doing shows, and nowadays everyone seems to have a podcast. (Pete has two—that's how easy it is.) So I get asked to be on a lot of podcasts. I often agree only to realize that I am now trapped in a small room with an exceptionally unstable person taping their first episode. I have started to research these podcasts in advance, and for the ones that don't meet my criteria (e.g., have been running at least a year), I say no—and now I am going to use Pete's method.

Will I write a joke here? No. Will I stop using the "I'm not going to write a joke here" joke as an excuse to not write a joke? Unfortunately, I am unable to do it.

EPILOGUE

THE CASE AGAINST COMEDIANS

At the outset of this book, I told you not to try to be funny like a comedian. I want you to *think* funny. To think differently. By now if I haven't changed your mind about the benefits of thinking like the masters of comedy, I never will.

But if I have changed your mind, you may still have reservations about using comedians as role models. Good for you.

While we can absolutely glean insights from these truly strange, creative people—and the truly hard work they do to make their strange, difficult job look effortless, they've got their share of bad habits and failings, as humans and professionals, like all of us.

As much as I want you to use comedians as models, it will also be useful to look to comedians for what *not* to do.

Here are three ways you shouldn't behave like the typical comedian.

BLAMING THE AUDIENCE

One of the most infuriating situations involving comedians occurs when they're performing on stage, not getting laughs, and then blame the audience. It's one thing to blame the audience backstage in the green room, or afterwards at the bar to fellow comedians. But it's another to blame the audience to their face. Commenting to the crowd on how dumb they are for not laughing not only doesn't bring them around to your side, but it poisons the water for subsequent performers.

SHTICK FROM SHANE

Whenever an audience doesn't laugh at a joke and the comic says, "You'll get that one on the way home," I hope that on the comic's way home they get that the audience understood the unfunny joke just fine.

As a business, if customers aren't buying your solution, you can't blame them. That will certainly not solve your sales problem. As a professional, if you're not getting hired, don't blame the businesses. In both cases, look back on yourself. Ask yourself: why am I not getting the outcomes I want?

BEING UNDIFFERENTIATED

One of the challenges in comedy is that most comedians don't cut through a cluttered marketplace. Someone goes to a comedy club and has a great time but can't remember the headliner's name—or you remember a joke but not the comedian's name. This is akin to having a weak brand. And a weak brand makes you invisible next to the competition.

If we're really honest, even comedians aren't creating enough of a chasm.

The power of niching is the anecdote to a weak brand. By picking a narrow target and leaning into that, you set yourself apart and become memorable to your target audience. Because the first hurdle is getting people to know that you exist.

People often look down on them, but comedians who have a shtick are often extremely memorable: Carrot Top, Emo, Gallagher, Margaret Cho, Bill Maher, Wanda Sykes, Gilbert Gottfried, and Conan's hair. And they're memorable because they're *different*. Not better, and not different in some deeply insightful way, but noticeably different nonetheless.

What is the shtick that sets you apart?

SHTICK FROM SHANE

When I started, I could do really edgy material with an "aw shucks" Midwestern persona. I was pushing the boundaries as far as I could. At the time, that was still somewhat novel. Sarah Silverman and Dave Attell were big names, but many of the modern, edgy comics had yet to gain attention. Louis CK was just some unknown creep. Doug Stanhope was someone every comic loved but had seemingly burnt every bridge in the business. Daniel Tosh had only just released his first album. No one had yet heard of Bill Burr or Jim Jefferies.

By the time things started taking off for me, those guys were all becoming big names for their edgy material. Not only was boundary pushing no longer novel, but they were all doing it better than I could.

Luckily, I had already started to focus on things that were more specific to my interests. I shifted my focus toward comedy with science themes. I started a podcast called *Here We Are* which helped me get a lot of attention on other bigger podcasts. Now I tour full-time doing a live show with scientists and comedians called Stand Up Science. It has been much more fun, successful, and fulfilling than the standard run-of-the-mill comedy shows most of us have to do.

Aw, shucks. I found a niche.

BEING UNHEALTHY

Comedians are notoriously bad at taking care of themselves. They sleep weird hours, don't exercise enough, and they eat too much truck stop food.

It may be that they're not grounded enough in a regular routine. It may be that because hard living is part of the comedy culture, comedians feel they have to adopt that life to be part of that world. Moreover, there are perverse incentives in comedy: when bad things happen, you get to make a joke out of it. Mitch Hedberg said, "The more I f*ck up, the better my career goes."

How many comedians have we lost too soon because they weren't taking care of their health. The list is too long, but you know the names: John Candy, Chris Farley, Bernie Mac, John Belushi. RIP.

If you want to do creative work, it helps to be healthy and energized, especially if you're trying to make something exciting.

All your ideas won't matter if you're not here to execute them. It's a marathon, not a sprint.

SHTICK FROM SHANE

Once I got black-out drunk during back-to-back shows on St. Patrick's Day. I didn't even remember being on stage. I walked into the club the next day terrified. I had no idea what happened the night before. The staff came up to me raving that it was the best comedy they had seen all year. I was relieved. Then I was heartbroken. A comic's biggest goal in life is to be remembered. But I will never get to remember what I am told was my most memorable night on stage.

I actually quit drinking for years because the thought of blacking out on stage was such a wake-up call for me. The next year, I went back to the club sober.

I didn't get booked there again for some time.

My business is probably a little different than yours.

GET YOUR SHTICK TOGETHER

Remember our mantra: Business is hard. Business is hard. Business is hard.

But when you develop killer practices and perspectives like the Masters of Comedy, you differentiate yourself from the competition—robots, businesses, other meat sacks.

And strong differentiation—in your thoughts and actions—can make business *less* hard.

Let's take a quick recap of what we've covered:

- The enemy of creativity and innovation is the status quo—the rules that say *this* is the way it must be done. Your competitive edge is how well you can fight off the fear of loss in favor of the bold possibilities that lie outside your (and everyone else's) comfort zone.
- In Reverse It and Step out of the Stream, you learned ways to think differently and the power that comes from doing the opposite of what is expected. You learned ways to smash the status quo.
- In Create a Chasm, you learned that the way to truly stand out is taking your *Out of the Stream* to the extreme, leaving the haters behind and focusing on your true fans who love what you do.
- In Cooperate to Innovate, you learned that partnering up with people who are different can generate a special kind of magic. But it takes figuring out who you are, showing up honestly and fully, and encouraging others to do the same. You also learned perhaps the most difficult skill to master: listening.
- In Write It or Regret It, you learned the power of recording your ideas in writing, so that you can capture, clarify, and communicate your ideas to your audience. This could be cooperative creatives, clients, or customers. But sometimes your audience is simply you.
- In Work Hard or Hardly Work, you learned to be a

blacksmith. How to create and produce badass craftsmanship and better enjoy your work through Protect, Grind, and Release. And the power of presence leads you to flow state, which is fun.

- In Take a Bigger Stage you learned three ways you can take your brand/career/life to the next level: Bigger Place. Bigger Platform. Bigger Perspective. Sometimes the only way to grow is to stop doing what you're doing—even if it's working—and shift to somewhere or something else.

- And here, within this epilogue, you learned three ways that comedians missed the mark. It's essential to take ownership of your craft and results. If something doesn't work, don't blame others. Get back to work. Next, don't just make something good. Intentionally differentiate yourself from the competition. And above all else, none of this matters if you're not alive and kicking—make your mental health and wellness your number one priority. Say it with me, "Is my health #1?"

I encourage you to think about how you might truly implement these lessons. You spend a third of your life working. Make the most of it. The work you do, and the life you live, is for you as much as it is for others. We need your innovations. We need your joy. Your jokes are optional.

If you want to hear more of my shtick, I'd love to speak to your organization. I can even bring a team of comedians in to help solve your biggest problems.

Please go to PeterMcGraw.org to connect with me.

- Booking information
- Downloadable resources
- Podcast episodes
- Mailing list
- Goofy pictures of me trying to look serious

ACKNOWLEDGMENTS

I like to give advice. I like to take advice.

This book gives a lot of advice. However, behind the scenes, I took a lot of advice to make it happen. The following people get a bunch of credit but no blame for this project.

First, I would like to thank everyone who has helped me with the humor research and other academic work that shows up in this book. None of the humor research would have happened without Caleb Warren, my benign violation co-creator. Caleb is everything you want in a co-author: kind, hardworking, well-read, whip smart, and has great taste in music. He has also been incredibly tolerant of me slacking on our academic papers while I wrote this book.

Thank you to the people whose projects, co-developed ideas, or perspectives show up herein: Lawrence Williams, Elissa Guralnick, William Kuskin, Phil Fernbach,

Anika Stuppy, Stephanie Tully, Leaf Van Boven, Jeff Larsen, and Janet Schwartz.

I can't thank enough my academic mentors: Barbara Mellers and Phil Tetlock. They believed in me and were patient as I figured out how to be not bad at research.

Adam Barsky was the only person who was willing to tell me that this book was a bad idea. Yes, I ignored your advice, but it pushed me to make something non-embarrassing. I hope you don't get to say, "I told you so."

Four generous people read early drafts of the manuscript. Thank you Ethan Decker, Mariah Baerend, Jay Mays, and Rachel Beisel for reading and giving critical yet encouraging feedback. Ethan, especially, was kind enough to provide incredibly valuable editorial and conceptual assistance.

I would have never written this book without having worked with Joel Warner on *The Humor Code*. He has taught me tons about writing, storytelling, and notetaking. Thanks, man.

There are too many people to mention who have helped with the production of the book. Most notably, I want to thank Kimberly Kessler. I couldn't have done this without you. You are a star! Thank you, also, Ellie Cole, Emily

Anderson, Jenny Shipley, and everyone else at Scribe Media and Lioncrest. Thank you Chris Denson for the introduction.

Thank you to the University of Colorado and the Leeds School supporting my sabbatical request, especially Sharon Matusik, John Lynch, and Laura Kornish. I *really* needed the time to get the book wrapped.

I appreciate the research and design help of Joe Harvey, Ashley DeCurtis, Kendall Carroll, Mathew Klickstein, Jeremy Sender, Steffen Baerend, and Mariah Baerend.

Lots of people were kind enough to appear on my podcast, give me interviews, or simply talk through the ideas, cases, research, and anecdotes. Here they are in no particular order: Caleb Warren, Steph Tully, Anika Stuppy, Luisa Diez, Jason Zinoman, Todd Glass, Neal Brennan, Barnet Kellman, Alonzo Bodden, Peter Murane, Darwyn Metzger, Jillian Lakritz, Bob Mankoff, Wendy Wood, Anita Woolley, Phil Fernbach, Bart de Langhe, Stefanie Johnson, Alex Gregory, Danielle Perez, Steve Stoliar, Adam Alter, Jeff Leitner, Jon Levy, Brad Bernthal, Richard Lewis, Briar Goldberg, Jack Shih, Linda Babcock, Laura Kornish, David Nihill, Dana Noffsinger, Josh Linkner, Jeff Mosenkis, Ivan Aristeguieta, Jen Overbeck, John Wenzel, Julie Seabaugh, Mark Sanborn, Mathew Klickstein, Will Hines, Billy Merritt, Mike Reiss, Tony Horton, Chris Mazzilli,

Natalie Shure, Dana Noffsinger, Natalie Barandes, Ethan Decker, Troy Campbell, Sarah Zaslow, Scott Paskoff, Stephen Morrison, Zach Hale, Gracie Koester, Anne-Laure Sellier, Lauren Alweis, Kaiwei Tang, Adrian Smith, Adrian Botan, Lam Helmick, Chuck Roy, Rick Fleenor, Jen O'Donnell, and Kim Kessler. My apologies if I left you out.

One group was especially helpful by giving me early feedback, ideas, and encouragement. Thank you, Matt de Caussin, Angel Lam, Charlie Merrill, Rachel Beisel, Anthony Full, James Craig, Dan Goldstein, Michael Sargent, and Dan Ariely.

An important group of people were supportive in innumerable ways behind the scenes. They are friends, mentors, and more: Darwyn Metzger, Mark Ferne, Jonathan Levav, Sheila Paxton, Julie Nirvelli, Shannon Sorino, and Mary Dahm. (And thanks to anyone who made me a cappuccino during this time.)

Finally, a very special thanks to Shane Mauss who is the star of this book. He has been a great friend, generous collaborator, and is a good guide if you ever want to do mushrooms.

I appreciate all of you.

Onwards!

ABOUT THE AUTHOR

DR. PETER MCGRAW is a behavioral economist, professional speaker, and expert on the scientific study of humor.

A marketing and psychology professor at the University of Colorado Boulder, McGraw investigates the interplay of emotions, judgment, and choice. His research has been covered by *The New York Times*, *Wall Street Journal*, NPR, BBC, *TIME*, CNN, *Wired*, and *Harvard Business Review*.

McGraw teaches graduate courses in behavioral economics for the University of Colorado Boulder and MBA courses in marketing management for London Business School, University of California San Diego's Rady School, and University of Colorado Boulder. He speaks at Fortune 500 companies, public events, and universities around the world.

As the director of the Humor Research Lab (aka HuRL), he has spent more than a decade examining the antecedents and consequences of humor. In 2014, he co-authored *The Humor Code: A Global Search for What Makes Things Funny*. McGraw has written for *Slate*, *Wired*, *Fortune*, *Huffington Post*, and *Psychology Today*.

McGraw hosts *I'M NOT JOKING*, a podcast that looks at the lives of funny people from entertainment, business, science, and the arts. He also hosts *Funny or True?*, a live comedy gameshow that pits comedians against scientists to see who has the best blend of brains and funny bone.

He is currently assisting a production company to develop a TV show based on his life.

Made in the USA
Monee, IL
03 December 2020